With the benefit of

A busman's life

by Bob Hind

*Dedicated to my wonderful wife Barbara
my support through it all*

Contents

Photographic Credits

Unless shown with the attribution listed below, the photographs in this book are from my own personal collection. I am grateful to the following photographers for providing their work.

AEJ Ted Jones
BB   Bernard Burrows courtesy of David Cole
BR   Bob Rowe
DC   David Cole
GL   Geoff Lumb
IS   Ian Stubbs
JH   John Hardacre courtesy of David Cole
JR   John Robinson
JS   John Senior
NBC National Bus Company courtesy Kithead Trust
PA   Paul Abell
RM   Roy Marshall
STA Senior Transport Archive

Chapter 1 – Early Beginnings

Someone once said that it must be in the blood to be in this business. Throughout the history of the bus industry, small companies have been handed from father to son; larger companies have seen the same names pass through their ranks, suggesting that a career in the bus industry might even be hereditary, if your ancestors had been smitten before you. In my case, the dynasty was once removed but no less strong and from both sides of my family tree. My paternal great grandfather had been a bus conductor on horse drawn trams in Fulham, in the 1890s, and an Inspector in Birmingham twenty years later. My maternal grandfather had been an electric tram driver. He had come from mid-Wales, at the start of last century, to the industrial Midlands to find work; which he did, and a family, and in time one of his sons followed him into a long career with the Corporation Transport Department.

I was born in that uncle's sitting room, so probably caught the bug there, and while there would be many opportunities to defy the inevitable, my closeness to my uncle in those early years decreed that I was destined to be a busman.

It was 1950, I had a ration card from birth; the country was still recovering from war. The bus industry was on the threshold of its most lucrative period in history; the transport infrastructure was fundamental to the re-building of the post-war generation. I was too young to experience the halcyon days of the early 'fifties but many an operator recorded its best and most profitable period in those years and, whilst they are now a distant memory to most, a few still mourn their passing.

In my home town of West Bromwich, the blue/green and cream buses were to impress themselves on my early years. The intrusion of the dark blue and cream ones confused; the trespass of the dowdy red ones foretold, although I was blissfully unaware, a large part of my destiny.

My earliest recollections of West Bromwich Corporation Transport Department are many and varied but perhaps the most distinctive was the numbers. I am told that I learnt to count from reading the route numbers, which is worrying as WBCT never had a route 13 so my elementary arithmetic was somewhat flawed. The destination blinds also complemented my reading practice, although I am still waiting to find 'Stone Cross', 'Tantany' or 'Friar Park' in one of the nation's literary masterpieces.

At an early age, I could match the number and destination and looking back I think I could have been an asset to the Department, if only they could have found a uniform small enough to fit me. I certainly remembered pestering my uncle to take me to the garage in Oak Lane and one Sunday my persistence paid off. He sat me behind the wheel of one of the buses I had always ridden on, but on which there was always a screen between the driver and me. Now I was the driver and I was hooked.

I have never been able to recall or understand different vehicle types. This account is not destined to be the essential manual for the enthusiastic bus-spotter, but the buses that remain most vivid in my childhood memories are undoubtedly those I saw in West Bromwich and one in particular which I will come to in due course.

It was the era of open back double-deckers. The West Bromwich fleet was dominated by Daimlers and the pride of that fleet was used on the Corporation's

If transport was in my blood, it could perhaps be traced back to my Great Grandfather, who worked on London's horse trams.

Although I did not remember the famous junction at Carters Green in West Bromwich in trams days, it did not change much as I grew up. Here four Birmingham City Transport trams can be seen at the location, carrying route numbers that were still carried by the West Bromwich buses when they took over jointly the replacing services in 1939. The Tower Cinema was to the left of the picture.

Twenty Daimler double-deckers were supplied to West Bromwich Corporation in 1952 and rather surprisingly were fitted with Weymann bodies, rather than the Corporation's preferred supplier, Metro-Cammell. Number 171 is seen here in the High Street, having just left the terminal point in Lower Queen Street and working on one of the joint services with Midland Red, the 220 to Bearwood. *(RM*)

When the trams through West Bromwich were replaced by buses in 1939, West Bromwich ordered 30 Daimler COG6s as its contribution to the replacement services. Nearly 20 years later, No. 84 is also seen in the High Street, still working on one of the tramway replacement services, the 74 to Dudley. *(RM)* .

longest route, the 74 from Birmingham to Dudley. The 74, on which I travelled regularly, epitomised most of the eccentricities that would endear WBCT to me for years to come. It was operated jointly with the big boys of the municipal world, Birmingham City Transport, yet, despite the 'agreement', the boundary line between the two Councils, at the Hawthorns, the home of West Bromwich Albion Football Club, was strictly observed. The ritual of crossing the boundary on each journey was only missing barbed wire and a customs post. There were no through fares, anyone wanting to cross the border paid again. The bus just waited outside the football ground while the conductor collected the fares and issued the tickets for the second time.

There were many landmarks along the route of the 74. The Birmingham terminus was outside the old Snow Hill Station, a mass of wrought iron and cobbled stones, with an air of not actually belonging to the City Centre. Snow Hill's history was a little cruel. It lost both its trains and its buses for a while, certainly lost its dignity when given a 'nineties makeover but it did finally have its status restored when the trains returned and it was given the unique distinction of being the Birmingham terminus for the return of the tram . . . for a while. Once over the boundary, the approach to West Bromwich town centre always seemed to me to be the longest, straightest, and possibly the widest piece of road in the world. It passed Salters, the famous weighing scales manufacturers, and entered High Street that was really all there was to the Town Centre.

The A41 trunk road was the town's spine; at the end of High Street it reached Carters Green, the parting of the ways – fork right for Wednesbury and Wolverhampton, left for Great Bridge and Dudley and in the fork, the Farley Clock Tower, dedicated to Reuben Farley, the first Mayor of West Bromwich. Someone with a sense of humour must have been responsible for this tower, whose sombre brickwork contrasted with the cinema hoardings opposite and, despite its sole purpose, always told the wrong time!

Although Carters Green was a principal timing point for the 74, conductors did not have to rely on the Clock Tower for punctuality. The Corporation provided its own time clocks, the Bundy clock, into which the conductors turned their keys before departing. This usually meant a lengthy wait that could be very frustrating as the stop we used to visit my aunt and uncle was immediately before Carters Green and often we could see the bus we had just missed waiting its time beneath the Clock Tower.

The route between Carters Green and Dudley seemed to be less densely urban (it wasn't) but it was probably an illusion caused by an absurdly wide carriageway, which made the pavements distant and the buildings more so. Across the railway lines, at Swan Village, along another stretch of cobbles, over the canal at the grandly named Great Bridge, under the railway bridge at Dudley Port to the Burnt Tree Island. There, in front of the Roman Mosaic building, our road joined the Birmingham New Road, which has been 'new' for over fifty years.

The final landmark was as near to the centre of Dudley that my grandfather and the trams ever got, so there must have been ghosts here that watched me each time I passed this way. On the whole route from Birmingham to Dudley it was unlikely that you would have seen a red bus but now, on the final approach to Dudley, that was to change dramatically. The castle looked down at you from its hilltop where you could just make out the cages of Dudley Zoo but to get there you had to pass the red buses on either side; in the 'Red' garage to your left and the coach park on your right. The trams never made it past this point, the final hill in front of them too much, but the bus services were eventually allowed to struggle up and into Fisher Street; there was the stronghold.

Fisher Street bus station was actually three roads, in the shape of a figure four, on the side of a very steep hill. The Birmingham and Midland Motor Omnibus Company Ltd (BMMO), or Midland Red as it was familiarly known, swarmed all over this hill. A hill that had proved almost disastrous on more than one occasion, when buses had rolled away, without their drivers. This was Midland Red territory and the Corporation buses were allowed to squeeze in on the end of one of the roads (they were even allowed to erect a key clock) but I firmly believe they only felt safe in Fisher Street because they were there in pairs. There was always one on the stand as another arrived. Fisher Street looked like an army encampment of red and any shade of blue was tolerated only momentarily.

Back in West Bromwich this situation was markedly reversed. Midland Red was only allowed into the town centre on joint services 220, 221 to and from Bearwood – the BMMO capital. WBCT buses in Bearwood looked like potato plants in a rose garden but in West Bromwich the Corporation pulled rank. Not only were the 'Friendly', as my uncle called them, with a hint of sarcasm in his voice – a reference to their branding ' the friendly Midland Red' – not allowed in the High Street, they were not allowed in the main terminus used by other WBCT routes. They were relegated to Lower Queen Street that was shared with the other joint services (14 and 54) WBCT ran with Walsall Corporation. And just to show that WBCT discriminated fairly, the only joint service operated by Wolverhampton Corporation (service 90), despite its municipal links, was concealed in Upper Queen Street on its own.

There was no bus station in West Bromwich in those days. Local services showed 'Dartmouth Square' as their terminal point. This was a slight deception as only through buses actually stopped in Dartmouth Square. The main stands were in Paradise Street close to the shopping centre and railway station – integration is nothing new. The imposition of a ring road and the building of a real bus station in the mid70s destroyed this arrangement and also the centre of the town. Ironically, the Corporations had the last laugh over the great Midland Red as by then they had combined to form part of the West Midlands Passenger Transport Executive (WMPTE) that had also absorbed the central core of the BMMO operations.

WBCT was very selective, almost discriminatory, in which of its own routes got the better (newer) buses. Routes to the east of the town, Stone Cross, the new Yew Tree Estate, Sutton Coldfield and Aldridge definitely got the better deals. The Cinderella services were certainly 15, 16 and 17. This was a cross-town route, although it remained on the west side of the town, linking Oldbury with Spon Croft. As a child watching these very square-looking buses, some pre-war, convinced me that these areas were decidedly second-class. The sharp lines of their bodies gave them a look of anger at having to plough the same route every day and not being allowed into Paradise Street.

Journeys between Birmingham and West Bromwich crossed the boundary at The Hawthorns, where one of the famous bundy clocks was sited. Here, Birmingham 2180, a Leyland-bodied Leyland PD2 waits for the clock to be 'pegged' before continuing on its journey to Wednesbury. *(BR)*

One of the wartime utilities, No. 124, still has its original Brush body, albeit substantially reconstructed by the Corporation in 1954. Even this was insufficient to significantly prolong its life, and a completely new body was provided by Alexander. The bus was operating on the comparatively short service number 30 to Greets Green. *(RM)*

During my time living in West Bromwich the No. 28 Circular service utilised rear-entrance single-deckers. After we had moved to Dudley the 28 service continued to be operated with rear-entrance single-deckers, but in this case unusually fitted to Leyland Tiger Cub chassis. Number 213 was one of three similar buses delivered in 1958, the choice of the bodybuilder also unusual, being provided by Mulliner, who were based in Birmingham and who, more usually, bodied military vehicles.*(RM)*

Typical of the single-deckers to which I referred above was No. 156, a Daimler CVG5 with Metro-Cammell 38-seat body. It is seen here in the High Street operating on the third joint service with Midland Red, the 252 to Smethwick.

West Bromwich Corporation took delivery of large numbers of Daimler CVG6s with Metro-Cammell bodies, both 27ft and 30ft long. One of the former, No.229, was delivered in 1960. Note the advert for the local building society. The conductor is engaged in conversation with the driver whilst changing the destination blind.*(BB)*

The terminus of the joint route to Wolverhampton was situated in the other part of Lower Queen Street. Wolverhampton No. 551, a Guy Arab with Park Royal 56-seat body stands at this rather remote location on the other side of the High Street. Note the unusual WBCTD bus stop. *(BR)*

The Dudley terminus of the trolleybus service 58 from Wolverhampton was based in Stone Street, another slightly remote location when compared with the other bus services in the town. Sunbeam W No. 437 was one of the first models of that marque supplied to Wolverhampton after the war and was originally fitted with a Park Royal body. It is seen here with a replacement Roe body.

The 58 trolleybus service passed through Sedgley, where this view was taken, and close to my new home, so there was the opportunity for the family to use this route. Wolverhampton No. 448, a Sunbeam W model had been delivered in 1948 but had its original Roe body replaced with a new one from the same manufacturer in the early 1960s.

My paternal grandmother lived on the north-east side of the town, near All Saints Church where many routes converged, which meant a visit opened the opportunity to travel on a wide selection of services and buses. Shamelessly, my allegiance was not to my local operator but to the blue buses of Walsall Corporation. These were Leylands and Guys, very different to the Daimlers which I was used to and they had one unique feature. Modern buses had an electric push button bell to stop and start the bus. Walsall buses had a bell cord. The cord produced a dull 'clunk' sound behind the driver's left ear that delighted me.

There is something magical about ringing bus bells; even in my later life, when I should have known better, I confess that I tried them on every new type of bus I encountered. My dream was fulfilled at a very early age, when we were travelling back to Dudley one evening, from a visit to relatives, and a kindly conductress let me work the bell all the way from Great Bridge. At eight years old I had decided to be a bus conductor and the intervening school years would only be an unnecessary inconvenience. I would follow in my uncle's footsteps and work from the Oak Lane garage as soon as I was old enough. Little did I know that, when I was old enough to get my licence, WBCT would be no more.

Whilst remembering visits to relatives, one of my aunts lived in Dagger Lane. This will mean nothing to anyone living outside West Bromwich, but to visit meant a ride on service 28 – the Outer Circle – operated by rear-entrance 38-seated Daimler single decks. To a child fascinated by buses these were truly enchanting. I didn't know where the 28 went, it seemed to serve roads that didn't deserve anything better, but the elderly vehicles toiled endlessly in circles and whichever way they went, you always ended at my aunts.

We had moved to Dudley in 1955 that, whilst it created many opportunities to travel on the 74 to visit relatives in West Bromwich, introduced two new bus experiences to add to my already growing collection. We lived near Eve Hill close to the Sedgley route to and from Wolverhampton. A Midland Red service passed the end of our road, but a walk (uphill) to the main road meant the journey, into Dudley town centre, could be made by the green and yellow Sunbeam trolleybuses of Wolverhampton Corporation. I say to the town centre but, just as with the 90 in West Bromwich, again, Wolverhampton's best did not quite make it and had their terminus in Stone Street: a cobbled square with a long wooden shelter and little else. True, it was only a few minutes walk to the shops but it always seemed isolated and lonely. There were still many sections of the 58 route out of Dudley that were cobbled and unlike their diesel cousins, trolleybuses seemed made to glide over them.

I'm not sure if we had moved to the poor side of town but even our BMMO service was an outsider. The D6 (we had now graduated from numbers to the alphabet – 'D' for Dudley – as well) linked Gornal Wood to Oakham (as D7) via Dudley. In consequence, the D6 was relegated to bus stops outside the main centre and was not even allowed into Fisher Street. This meant that at the end of a visit to West Bromwich we were faced with a walk from the bus station to the square bus stop in Union Street. No shelter, little light and in a winter's mid-evening, arctic. It was, however, a more than welcome sight when the big red bus appeared round the corner of Union Street.

In the two years we lived in Dudley, I never saw where the 58 trolleybus ended after it had left me at Eve Hill, never stayed on the D6 to Gornal Wood bus station and although Fisher Street was a treasure trove of red routes waiting to be discovered, it was the 74 that was ever our sole reason to visit.

When I was seven we moved west. Looking back it was a great adventure, moving into the countryside (admittedly to a newly built housing estate) and away from the urban sprawl and brewery smells of Dudley. Nowadays it is probably a ten minute drive through an area densely housed that gives no indication where urban ends and country begins. But in 1957 we travelled through fields and open countryside to reach our new semi-detached home in Wall Heath. We had also moved back into Staffordshire from Worcestershire, which was strange to a seven year old as we were still not far, barely ten miles, from my Staffordshire birthplace.

The new estate was built alongside the main Wolverhampton – Kidderminster A449 road, although Wall Heath was also the junction for those wishing to visit Stourbridge. The village centre was a ten minute walk from my new house and, for the first year, was where my primary school, opposite the church, was located. As the estate grew the need for its own school also grew and I subsequently transferred to Maidensbridge County Primary School. The village's principal bus service was the 261 whose terminus at the end of the village was in a large council estate ominously named Blaze Park. The 261 went to Dudley so was our main link with civilisation and the 74 back to West Bromwich. In fact the 261 stopped opposite the 74 in Fisher Street so the era of waiting in poorly lit side streets had passed.

The newcomers on the Holbeache Estate, however, had the additional advantage of being adjacent to the Wolverhampton – Stourbridge corridor and therefore the use of service 882 (or 885 when it occasionally extended to Kidderminster). Amazingly, these routes totally ignored the centre of Wall Heath village and continued along the main road as if it didn't exist. It was some years later that this was rectified.

The other new experience was to be the 883. This was also a route that linked, albeit infrequently, Wolverhampton and Kidderminster but travelled through Kinver and past the Stewponey Hotel. Whilst the hotel was of no significance, behind it was an outside swimming pool. A popular local attraction in the summer although slightly less so when we were bussed from school for compulsory swimming lessons which began each year in March! The 883 was also my first experience of BMMO single decks and fired my enthusiasm to explore more widely.

At 11 my education moved to the Grammar School outside Brierley Hill which meant travel by bus – the 882 – and, until numbers warranted a bespoke school bus, a long uphill walk up Bromley Lane. When the school bus eventually appeared, much to the relief of most of the adult travellers on the 882, we were taken door to door but subjected to a much more disciplined journey. I am not certain whether the staff at Midland Red's Hartshill depot drew lots to avoid this particular school bus but we were usually blessed with the cream of their 'no-nonsense' employees. One particular platinum blonde conductress, as wide as she was tall, enjoyed swinging her Setright ticket machine a she patrolled the aisles. This must have been the quietest school bus in the whole of the Midlands.

Now that I was allowed to travel to and from school by bus it was only a short step to persuade my parents I was old enough to venture further afield and explore

West Bromwich 171, one of 20 Daimlers CVG6s with Weymann bodies delivered in 1952, overtakes a Midland Red D7 double-decker in Lower Queen Street operating on the joint 220 service to Bearwood. *(BR)*

Parked at the rear of West Bromwich Corporation's Oak Lane premises is Daimler single-deck number 156, new in 1952. Note the unusual 'Edinburgh style' rear-entrance. After withdrawal in 1967 it passed into local preservation and is still to be seen at rallies nearly 50 years later! *(BR)*

Most of Midland Red's double-deckers were built by themselves at their Carlyle works, but there were exceptions. A small batch of Guy Arabs with bodies built by Guy on Park Royal frames were allocated type GD6. Originally these had Meadows engines but were later fitted with BMMO K-type engines. These were based in the Wolverhampton/Dudley area, and this example, No.3563, is seen here in Dudley. *(STA)*

An example of the output of Carlyle works is this D7, No. 4432, with Metro-Cammell body, parked in Dudley bus station alongside a sister vehicle in 1968. *(BR)*

A further, and much larger, exception to the 'home-built' rule was the delivery of 100 Leyland PD2s to Midland Red. Number 3997 is seen on service 885 which, as mentioned in the text, passed through Stourbridge on its way to Kidderminster.

Pre-war Midland Red operated a large fleet of front entrance double-deckers, which in its inimitable pragmatic way were designated 'FEDD'. These iconic buses had virtually all disappeared from service by the time I had become familiar with the company's area, but for nostalgia's sake No. 2254 is included here.

what Midland Red had to offer beyond Wall Heath. Their 'Day Anywhere' ticket was to open up a whole new world. For just five shillings (25p) I could explore the Midland Red empire from Northampton to Shrewsbury, from Hereford to Nottingham. And I did, every holiday, often dragging an unwilling friend with me. Immediately after my twelfth birthday, at the beginning of the long summer break, I set off on my travels.

The object of these excursions was to cover as much ground in one day as possible (which I did); to visit the outer regions of the BMMO empire, and therefore the Midlands (which I did); to stretch my day to its extreme so that I would get the maximum benefit of my five shillings investment, which I also did.

There were occasions when I was not totally in control of my itinerary. My last excursion before, in Midland Red's view, I reached adulthood, could have ended in disaster. It was April 1966, I set out early with a friend to explore the southwest reaches of the network that required some careful preparatory scheduling as the services in the Hereford and Ross-on-Wye area tended to be infrequent and complicated. All was going according to plan as we travelled through Stourbridge and Worcester to Hereford. As we neared Hereford in the late morning, it began to snow.

Any sensible young men would have realised the impending risks and headed homeward at the next opportunity; but, intrepid as ever, we decided to press on, catching our connection from Hereford to Fownhope, from where we intended to travel to Ross-on-Wye. The 478, an elderly BMMO single-deck with no appreciable heating, did appear but as the weather worsened the journey got longer and more seriously, later. By the time we reached Ross-on-Wye, it was obvious we had missed our connection back to Ledbury from where we had intended to return to Worcester. We were the only two passengers dropped in Ross, and in fact our bus, which was now disappearing into the snowstorm, seemed to be the only movement, human or vehicular in the town. We crossed to the Ledbury stop hoping to find an alternative solution to frostbite, when the bus that had recently left us, re-appeared through the gloom, displaying '472 Ledbury'. It hadn't got any warmer while it had been turning round, but we were never more pleased to see it. The driver courageously battled through to Ledbury, where the bus to Worcester was waiting and we were delivered safely homeward.

So, my 'Day Anywhere' tickets introduced me to such exotic locations as Coalville, Swadlincote and Tamworth, locations that were to become a much more significant part of my life sooner than I might have expected. My trips started to hone my scheduling skills that, much to the frustration of those later employed by me, were always my most treasured achievement.

My teenage explorations were not confined to the Midlands. On holiday in Bournemouth, I discovered that Hants and Dorset also had a 'Day Out' ticket that enabled me to visit Salisbury, Winchester and Southampton, although I had to pay the full adult fare of ten shillings (50p). Our family holidays always gave me the opportunity to experience other bus companies, names that have long since disappeared or been absorbed in to big groupings. Our trips to mid and South Wales introduced me to Western Welsh from Llangranog and Aberporth to Newcastle Emlyn. In Tenby, Silcox Motors intrigued me with its bespoke (irregular) timetables.

17

At 16 I was old enough to start working on Saturdays at Woolworths in Stourbridge for the princely sum of £1 per day. It was eight hours slave labour stacking shelves and did not endear me to working for a living. Stourbridge was where my father was born although trips for shopping were usually to Dudley and Wolverhampton. The terminus for most Midland Red services in Stourbridge was actually in their bus garage in Foster Street although some services struggled up an incredibly steep incline to the station forecourt opposite the bus depot.

I was 17, with one year to complete before sitting my A levels, when my parents decided they wanted to start a new life by opening a bed and breakfast business in Llandudno. It was an opportune time to move my younger sisters but I was the problem. The decision was made that I should stay with my aunt and uncle, who by now was Assistant Traffic Superintendent at West Bromwich Corporation Transport Department. The decision to spend a year with my favourite uncle was a bonus to the prospect of adolescent freedom. So in September 1967, I was abandoned by the rest of my family and started my lodging in Stone Cross, on the Walsall side of my birthplace.

At first, travelling to school in Brierley Hill from Stone Cross was a novelty as it involved three bus journeys: Stone Cross to Wednesbury, Wednesbury to Brierley Hill then from the town centre out to the Grammar School on Bromley Lane. As with my 'Day Anywhere' adventures, I soon learnt that bus connections were not always reliable and as the winter set in my enthusiasm for regular bus travel waned. By Christmas my father was persuaded that I needed some wheels of my own. Fortunately it was too far to cycle, so I was given a small Honda 50 motorbike, which immediately enhanced my freedom and diminished my attention to schoolwork. My mock A levels were due to start in February and, in all honesty, I was ill-prepared having been greatly distracted by social engagements.

My journey home to Stone Cross would usually take me through Dudley across Burnt Tree Island towards Dudley Port. On the evening before the start of my exams, I was travelling along this section, in the gloom of the dusk, when a van emerged from a side road. I collided with it, was thrown over its top and woke up with a major headache in Dudley General Hospital. There is no doubt my crash helmet saved my life; the headache continued for several weeks but I escaped the embarrassment of my mocks.

About once a month I ventured on British Rail to visit my parents in their new North Wales home but my experience of long waits and poor connections on Crewe station did not endear me to the rail industry. My evenings and weekends away from parental control were given over to socialising at the expense of any serious educational work. My dedication to the pursuit of good A level results had completely dissipated. Whilst my friends had planned their college and university paths, I had no inclination for further education. Not surprisingly, I failed my A levels and reached the summer of 1968 with six O levels and a decision to make – what to do next?

Chapter 2 – The Crosville Years

I knew I wanted a career in transport (although I was not certain what that meant) and I knew that I would like to be in buses but my options, now that I was to live in Llandudno, seemed somewhat limited. So I searched for transport management schemes and, despite my limited educational achievements, received invitations for interviews from three of the four applications I made. I travelled to London for entrance examinations with both British European Airways and British Rail and to Manchester for an interview with the haulage giant, British Road Services. The application into which I had put the most energy and enthusiasm was to my local bus company, Crosville. In time, to my amazement, BEA, BR and BRS all offered me an opportunity to join them, but, to my great disappointment, Crosville declined my overtures, saying that they were not taking on any more trainees at that time.

Despite that knock back, I had to opt for some sort of employment so, for some inexplicable reason that still escapes me, I accepted the offer from the hauliers, British Road Services. Actually, I think it was because they were based in Manchester and the other two were London based, but haulage had never been high on my list of transport interests. The BRS management scheme was due to start in early September 1968, so I had a whole summer in front of me to occupy. I knew that Crosville employed seasonal conductors along the North Wales coast, so I applied to my nearest depot, at Llandudno Junction, for temporary employment. For the second time Crosville rejected me, but this time for quite legitimate and legal reasons. I was still 17, would not be 18 until 12th July so I was not deemed old enough to hold a conductor's licence. However, this time my disappointment was short-lived when, to fill the two weeks before I became of age, they asked me to work in the Conwy office as a parcel boy.

The Crosville network spread across North and Mid-Wales to Lancashire and Cheshire and parcel delivery by bus was a flourishing trade, often quicker and cheaper than the Post Office. Newspapers used the service, car parts to groceries – most deliveries guaranteed the same day. So the parcel boy's role was to meet the appropriate bus either to collect an incoming parcel or to despatch one.

The Conwy office was actually a very small shed located opposite the main westbound stop in Lancaster Square. It normally housed (and only had room for) its resident occupant, Inspector Albert Evans. Albert Evans was as much a part of the Conwy infrastructure as a Crosville employee. He was well known to all the locals and many of the regular seaside visitors and enjoyed his fame without too much exertion.

The arrival of a young lad to undertake most of the exercise was, therefore, a welcome opportunity for Albert to relax in the July sun. In the quiet moments, he was an entertaining storyteller and within a few days of our acquaintance, I was learning the industry's innermost secrets. As a sideline we sold a few timetables, booked some excursions and stood in the sunshine passing the time of day with anyone who wanted to pass it with us. My first introduction to the bus industry was therefore very leisurely. Because it was high summer, buses never ran on time – those from along the coast were sometimes several hours late – but Albert took this in his stride effortlessly placating potential passengers whilst the mounting traffic congestion became a backcloth to a holiday scene as idyllic as anywhere.

The two weeks passed too quickly, with little incident and plenty of gossip except for one occasion that clouded the laughter and enjoyment. One afternoon, a bus pulling into the kerb misjudged the manoeuvre, mounted the kerb wrenching the wheel from the driver's grip and pinned a waiting passenger to the railings behind the narrow pavement. My lasting memory of the incident was a burst bag of flour in the lady's shopping bag spilling like a waterfall on to the pavement. The lady was unharmed but at that moment, I started to appreciate the realities and the dangers of operating 10-ton vehicles.

On the day I became 18, I was introduced to my second Inspector, Johnny Roberts who, with one arm, was the most adept trainer of the use of the Setright ticket machine (yes, the one that had been so threatening on the school bus). He taught me the complexities of singles and returns, exchanges and emergencies and within a week I was ready to join one of the older Llandudno conductors who would keep a watchful eye over me as I was let loose on an unsuspecting public.

Banford Williams had one rule to being a good conductor. Never stand up when you can sit down. At which point he would sit himself on the bench seat at the rear of the bus and let me get on with the work. Obviously rule 44 did not apply to Banford. It said, 'The conductor's position on the Bus at all times when not collecting fares is at the main entrance of the Bus. Conductors must remain standing in built-up areas'. I proved a good novice, bought my share of the tea and within a week or so I was allowed to work on my own.

My first solo journey was on service M93 to Pant-y-tan, on a small single-deck which wound its way up the hills behind Conwy until it came to an abrupt halt alongside a post box, with no sign of any dwelling. I looked around and there was no sign of life anywhere, but my driver was in no rush to return. After what seemed an age, we reversed into a side road and waited; at least we were now facing from where we had come. I thought we were about to set off when I noticed a figure some distance away. A lady with a shopping basket eventually boarded and we immediately set off. I was to learn on many occasions after that, that our regulars were our most valued. This lady's travel habits, like so many others, were well known and she would never be left behind. The relationship between the Crosville staff and their locals, particularly in Wales, was legendary and this was true customer service at its best.

Even in the late 'sixties, foreign package holidays were still in their infancy so the popularity of the North Wales coast as the annual holiday destination had not yet diminished, particularly amongst the Brummies and the Scots. People who are on holiday are generally there with the intention of enjoying themselves and this made the conductors' job enviable.

The services between Rhyl, Colwyn Bay and Llandudno were packed with happiness and even learning to deal with the occasional happy drunk was a pleasure. Ploughing up and down, past the endless caravan sites and holiday homes with the occasional extension to Bangor and Caernarfon or even on the famous 'Cymru Coastliner' to Chester was magical and it took no persuasion to work 'doubles' – an early and a late shift on the same day – when your passengers enjoyed your company as part of their holiday.

Late shifts on the North Wales coast had their novelties. Because of the length of the route between Rhyl and Caernarfon, over 40 miles, it was impossible to easily schedule a bus back at night to the depot from where it had started in the morning. The easy solution was to let the buses finish where the service terminated and to change crews at a convenient point so that, at least, they would finish at home at the end of their shift. These crew changeovers could happen at any time during the day but the exciting ones were generally on the last journeys.

One such changeover was between crews from our depot at Llandudno Junction and our colleagues from Bangor on the last A1 journeys from Rhyl and Caernarfon. Whilst the changeover point was nominally somewhere around Llanfairfechan, the object was to meet up as quickly as possible so that we could get home before midnight. Once we had swapped buses, often in the middle of nowhere, the return journey to the depot was usually hair-raising. The coast road at that time was fairly narrow, weaving around overhanging rocks with the open rear platform of the bus perilously close to the sea side of the road. Standing on the platform was not advisable when your driver was setting a world record and there was only a low wall between you and the waves below. I cannot remember one instance of us arriving at the depot later than scheduled.

The services along the North Wales coast were a work of art. In the mid-'sixties a grand plan had been devised to link routes so that it would be possible to travel from Caernarfon to Chester without changing buses. Needless to say the summer traffic destroyed the theory of a perfect timetable and within weeks the service was split at Rhyl, with that depot sharing the westward leg with the two Llandudno depots, Bangor and Caernarfon and the eastbound leg with the depots at Flint and Chester.

The whole through link was still maintained by a coach-operated limited stop service branded the 'Cymru Coastliner' that operated hourly between Chester and Llandudno Junction extending two-hourly to and from Caernarfon. The timetables for these routes continued to be devised with little thought as to where vehicles (and crews) might start or finish. In consequence an elaborate vehicle graph was created to ensure that vehicles, that could be away from their home depot for days at a time, were properly maintained and crews chopped and changed vehicles along the route so that they ended their shift at their home depot.

That summer conducting was happiness itself and as the time to leave and start my new job in Manchester grew near, I began to have grave doubts that I wanted to do anything other than continue to be a bus conductor. The Depot Superintendent at Llandudno Junction was a kindly Lancastrian called Bill Barge. He ran the depot efficiently and with a quiet discipline but was well respected by all his staff. One day he called me into his office and told me that he knew that I had applied for the traffic management scheme and why didn't I try again. I told him that I had already accepted another position with British Road Services but he was undeterred and a few days later, while I was taking a break, he told me that I was to meet the Assistant Traffic Manager in the office at Colwyn Bay and he would re-interview me for the traineeship.

The meeting with TA (Algy) Elwyn was to be monumental. I had obviously managed to impress somebody during my short period at the Junction and our

Although Crosville had almost a monopoly of services in North Wales, Llandudno UDC ran a small fleet of single-deck buses which were used on tours of the town and also to the Great Orme. The interesting fleet included Guys and Fodens as seen above. (*BR}*

A mainstay for rural routes in the early post-war years were Bristol L models with Eastern Coach Works bodies, many of which lasted in service until NBC days. This example is a Gardner-engined LL model which is the 30ft variant, but still 7ft 6ins wide, and was delivered in 1950. The vehicle is ready to operate the route D17 from Wrexham to Moss. *(GL)*

Picturesque Caernarfon was the terminus for a number of North Wales Independent operators at one time, including Whiteway whose Bedford OB is seen here. *(BB)*

Perhaps less attractive aesthetically, but nevertheless as frequent a destination during my spell on the platform was Rhyl, where a local service is seen leaving the bus station.*(BR)*.

meeting culminated with him asking me if I would like to join the management scheme at the end of the summer. I never got to Manchester; I was not going to lose the opportunity of a career in the bus industry for a second time and so, early in September that year, I joined three other trainees to start my three years apprenticeship.

The scheme expected the trainee to work on every aspect of running buses from bus cleaning to head office policy. The depth of knowledge and experience and the wide geographical variation across the Crosville empire from which the trainee could learn, was probably unlike any other scheme in the country at that time.

My first period of training took place at my home depot at Llandudno Junction, in the cash office. Under the watchful eye of Dilys Hughes and Ernie the Chief Clerk, I quickly learned the daily administrative routine and, most importantly, how to add up continuity sheets. These were the opening and closing numbers of every ticket machine allocated to the depot. The opening number subtracted from the closing number was supposed to represent the amount of cash that should have been deposited by the conductors the previous evening. It never balanced so the continuity sheets were passed round the office until, at some point, someone would get the right answer. Dilys was the long-suffering mainstay in the office, quietly burdened with the male shortcomings but never rattled by anything – even the morning when Ernie, after a regular late night binge, appeared with only half of his moustache still attached to his upper lip.

With the fundamentals of office administration under my belt, it was quickly decided that I would benefit from a change of scenery. My transfer to Denbigh meant an hour and a half bus journey through Rhyl at the end of which was my first meeting with the formidable Miss Edna Pierce.

Denbigh was a small depot that ran country services in that part of Denbighshire and the mainline service between Rhyl and Denbigh that occasionally continued southwards to Rhuthin. Edna was designated 'Clerk-in-Charge' but in truth, she did and ruled everything. Everyone in Denbigh knew her and whilst, on our first meeting, she was slightly intimidating, in a small matter of time I realised how valuable her knowledge was and, more importantly, how friendly and supportive she was to be. I learnt much about running small depots and managing relationships from the formidable Miss Pierce. For the remainder of my first winter as a trainee, I worked between Llandudno Junction and Denbigh and in the early spring of 1969 my wages training took place in Rhyl to complete the first stage of running an office.

When I was informed that, at the end of April, I would be spending six months in Liverpool this came as something of a shock for two reasons. My aunt and uncle in West Bromwich apart, I had not lived away from home on my own and, furthermore, I was not sure that I was keen to leave my comfort zone in North Wales to move into the big city. In the event, it is no exaggeration to say that Liverpool was to change my life forever.

The reason I was being sent there was that Crosville operated a large network of express services across North and Mid-Wales and also between Liverpool and London. The depot at Edge Lane was the main hub for these services and all the planning and charting of the bookings made at offices and agents across the country was centred in Liverpool. Women (it was all female) employed in the chartroom recorded all bookings, and the number of vehicles required on each service each day was determined from these bookings. Not surprisingly, in the summer the activity intensified considerably with the annual pilgrimage of Liverpudlians to the North Wales coast. I was to learn how to run express services and private hire and all aspects of coaching during the peak season. I was not sure that this was a part of the industry that would interest me but my teachers were to change my attitude.

George Owen and Snowy Allen were legendary. They were closeted together in a small office in Edge Lane. George was nominally the boss but as he teetered on the edge of a heart attack daily, and Snowy was as laid-back as anyone could be; as exact opposites they managed, between them, to cope with the inevitable crises (and there were many). And because it was Liverpool, it was also inevitable that one was a Liverpool supporter and the other an Evertonian.

I was to stay with the family of one of the mechanics from Edge Lane and arrived in Old Swan at the end of April, the day before I was due to report to my two new bosses. Within minutes of my arrival I was told that I would not fit into this office unless I pledged allegiance to one of the two football clubs. I had always been interested in football. As a very young boy my father and grandmother had regularly taken me to the Hawthorns to watch West Bromwich Albion. Now however, I was in the big league and to this day I'm not certain why I chose Liverpool over Everton; perhaps it is because George was the boss although I think there was more to it than that. However, on that day in April 1968 I became a 'Red' and grew more loyal to the team over the following decades than I had ever imagined.

Whilst Liverpool was to give me my football team it was also to give me my wife, Barbara. The older women in the chartroom were used to mothering the trainees that appeared each summer and I was no exception but I was only interested in the girl who had come to augment the staff for the peak holiday season. Before the end of that year we were engaged and in the following summer married.

To say that operating express services from Liverpool to North Wales at the height of the summer holidays was chaotic would be an understatement in the extreme. Coaches and buses were brought in from all points and from a variety of operators to ferry the many hundreds of families to caravan sites, holiday camps and hotels along the coast. On summer Saturdays there were journeys that left first thing in the morning, in the hope that the buses would return in time to do another journey at lunchtime and, if we were really lucky, to do a third journey in the early evening. It rarely worked. Because of the exodus along the coast road, not only by bus passengers but cars as well, the morning departures were left with little chance of ever returning on time. In fact it was not uncommon for vehicles to return four of five hours later than they were scheduled.

This created a minor dilemma from mid-morning onwards as holidaymakers, expecting to embark on their journey to the sunshine at lunchtime, began to arrive at the Edge Lane terminal. As the departure time drew near, a very empty yard devoid of any sort of transport, now heaved with the holidaymakers. Initially, with the prospects of a sunny fortnight in Rhyl or Prestatyn, the atmosphere was always lively and cheerful but after a couple of hours, an element of concern started to set in.

Crosville had a quarterly magazine 'Crosville United' with news from each of its depots. My first appearance came at Christmas 1968.

Bill Barge was Depot Superintendent at Llandudno Junction who employed me as a Parcels Clerk and suggested that I try again for the traffic traineeship.

and the children from Blodwel home will again be invited.

Driver M. L. Blanchard and Conductor P. Drummond have left the Company's Service to take up other employment, and we wish them well.

We welcome to the Office Staff Mr. R. A. Hind who during the season was employed as a seasonal Conductor and is now a Traffic Trainee. We wish him every success and hope that he will make the grade and spend many happy years in the transport industry.

We also welcome Mr. Michael Goosey who is now an assistant in our Schedules Office.

To Meredith Davies, Assistant Schedules Clerk, and Mechanic S. A. Selby who are at present in

Finally, to all Crosville employees, we extend our best wishes in this festive season.

LLANDUDNO TOWN

As I write this the first frost of winter is on the ground. So far we have been very fortunate in having such mild weather.

We are all looking forward to Christmas and hope that you all have a happy time. The tempo of life has risen as Christmas draws near, and therefore we are getting very busy. I hope we will be able to continue this boom until well after Christmas as it's a long time before the spring visitors arrive.

Mr. W. E. Barge, who retired in July after 42 years service with Crosville.

Although he did not enjoy the best of health driving the last few years prior to his retirement, he never allowed it to interfere, or reflect on his scrupulously fair judgement.

One was immediately put at ease by his unbiased manner of handling staff, and company problems, whenever one was called to his office you could rest assured that you would get a fair hearing, if you were in the right he was 100% behind you, but woe betide the unsuspecting "rooky" who tried to "pull the wool" over his eyes, he knew every trick of the trade, and was too much a wise old owl to be fobbed off with fairy tales.

Mr. Barge, our Depot Superintendent for the past 23 years reached the age of 65 on 5th July, 1970, and retired after 43½ years service with the Company. He commenced as a Conductor at Chester in 1926, was promoted to Traffic Inspector, then moved to Crewe as Depot Superintendent in 1940 and finally to Llandudno Junction in 1947

Mr. T. A. ELWIN

Mr. T. A. Elwin previously Chief Assistant Traffic Manager was appointed Traffic Manager with effect from 1st March, 1972.

This must be a popular appointment as Mr. Elwin is well known to a large number of Crosville staff through his long association with the Company, dating from 1933, and I am sure I can count on everyone giving him their support in his new duties.

Mr. Elwin originally started in Mold, and after Army service in the Royal Army Service Corps where he attained the rank of Captain, he returned to Crosville with positions at Dolgellau, and Bangor when he moved to Wrexham in 1960 as Divisional Manager. He was appointed Assistant Traffic Manager (West) in June 1965 and in December 1970 became Chief Assistant Traffic Manager.

13.4.72.

General Manager.

Mr. T. A. Elwin

Algy Elwyn interviewed me at the back of the Colwyn Bay enquiry office and decided that I should become a management trainee.

My training involved relief spells at smaller depots. Denbigh was a favourite.

recent months and Denbigh was no exception. Indeed at one time it developed into a minor crisis, but fortunately the wheels were kept turning. Things are getting normal again thanks to Aspro and Asprin—The great little pill.

We are glad to see Conductor D. Mackie back on the platform also Garage Foreman R. T. Evans at his desk in the office.

To Drivers Tom Roberts and Isaac Edwards we send our best wishes for a speedy recovery, both are at present in hospital.

BIRTH

To Driver and Mrs. J. P. Jones a son — John Andrew. Our sincere congratulations and good wishes.

RELIEF VISITS

Mr. Robert Hind from Llandudno spent a few weeks with us as a holiday relief Clerk. He was well liked by everyone and we all join in wishing him a very successful career. What about a trip to Epworth, Robert?

FROM RHYL

Driver Gwilym A. Evans has joined us and we sincerely hope he will be happy in our ranks.

GOING ABROAD

After a long hard winter everyone looks forward to Summer holidays. Arrangements have already started and we are given to understand that our popular Wages Clerk, Miss E. E. Pierce, is visiting Canada. She is not emigrating. We wish her good flying, a memorable holiday and a safe return home. "We'll keep a welcome."

SHINING TALENT

Those who appreciate good music are very grateful to Harry Mechanic and Syd Jones of Rhyl for their fine rendering of classical music on Tuesday and Fridays.

Caernarfon was a popular tourist attraction and therefore generated a considerable amount of traffic for Crosville and I became acquainted with the town on a regular basis when I commenced conducting in 1968 The L1 Cymru Coastliner had been introduced in 1965 and linked Chester with Caernarfon. Crosville had purchased ten Bristol FLF double-deckers finished to coach specification for use on this service. The modifications include designated luggage accommodation at the rear of the lower saloon which meant the seating capacity of these buses was only 55. Originally delivered in all-over cream, the year I arrived they were repainted into green and cream express livery as seen here. *(GL)*

In April 1969 I was notified that I would be spending six months in Liverpool. Apart from time spent with relatives, this was the first time that I was to live away from home. Liverpool was such a change from North Wales and subsequent events were to change my life forever. Crosville's principal terminus was at the iconic Pier Head, where many of the City Transport's services were also found. A Bristol FLF is about to depart for Chester. As WJ Crosland-Taylor explained in his history of the company, 'The Sowing and the Harvest', the Merseyside area routes were vital for the financial wellbeing of the company.

Between 1958 and 1964 Crosville had taken delivery of 100 Bristol MW coaches with Eastern Coach Works bodies. One of the ten 39-seaters which were delivered in 1963, and also seen at Liverpool Pier Head, is CMG472 (2177 FM). *(GL)*

After 18 months of training I was required to act as holiday relief at Blaenau Ffestiniog. This Bristol SC was typical of the small allocation of buses to this depot. In later years some lost their cream relief as shown here. *(GL)*

As the junior in the office I was dispatched to keep the customers happy and informed. Quite simply this meant lying to them that their buses would appear very soon. When eventually they did, the air of relief was generally tinged by surprise, dismay or downright anger when our customers were confronted by the double-decker buses that many of them would have been using to and from work or school the previous week.

However, these vehicles would easily accommodate 60 or 70 people even though their luggage had to be piled on to the bench seats at the rear of the downstairs saloon. The conductors' duty, as conductors were used on these express services, was not only to ensure the passengers were all seated safely but to stand astride of the gangway supporting the luggage throughout the entire journey to ensure that suitcases and their contents were not scattered around the saloon. It was often frenetic, it was certainly chaotic but it was an enjoyable adventure and our passengers obviously did not suffer too much because they always returned to go through the same experience the following year.

The Edge Lane Depot Superintendent was Les Brereton and whilst his depot's claim to fame was being the centre of Crosville's express services, he also ran many of the local bus routes in and around the city. These were still the days when Liverpool Corporation provided the main local network but ancient agreements had allowed Crosville into the suburbs and, with Ribble Motor Services, the right to provide the inter-urban network.

Merseyside Passenger Transport Executive had been established the previous year and had already absorbed the municipal operations of Liverpool, Birkenhead and Wallasey. The full set would be completed with the addition of Southport and St Helens in 1974. I could never have imagined that, thirty years later, the resulting Merseybus network would be the subject of the biggest acquisition in which I would be involved.

My six months in the Coaching department soon ended. I had gained the football team, my future wife and also learned how to queue outside a public house at 5.25 in the evening, waiting for opening time. I had also learned what managing in the midst of chaos and crisis was all about. Far from being intimidated by the Scousers, they were welcoming and supportive and I grew to treat Liverpool as my second home. There is no doubt that over the years Liverpool has deserved some of its bad press and the 'sixties and 'seventies were not all good for the city but there was something in the underlying fabric of the place that suggested it would come through smiling and the Liverpool we know today deservedly ranks alongside some of the world's great cities.

Returning to Llandudno Junction I was to join the schedules office under the guidance of the Assistant Divisional Manager. Scheduling has always been my first love in this industry. There is some satisfaction in planning the services as efficiently as you can and seeing your efforts at work on the road. Bill Edwards, who was the ADM at the time, was a most proficient scheduler and a good tutor. Scheduling was done on a divisional basis and the divisional office at Llandudno Junction was responsible for the services of the two Llandudno garages (the Town and Junction depots), Rhyl, Denbigh and the outstation at Llanrwst. This was a time when everything was planned with the aid of a pencil and rubber and the hand written duty boards were duplicated by a Roneo machine and pasted on to a metal plate for the driver.

This was also my first experience of hierarchy in the divisional management set-up. The Divisional Manager at Llandudno was George Penketh, one of the nicest people and kindly managers I have ever met. His office was next to the schedules office, occupied by the ADM, two other clerks as well as myself. As the junior member of staff I was allocated four bells. If the divisional manager demanded your attention, the bells over his door rang once for his assistant twice or three times for the two clerks and (very rarely) four times for me.

During this period I got to work on the complicated coastal services – the A1 and A2 services between Rhyl, Llandudno and Caernarfon and the 'Cymru Coastliner' between Chester, Llandudno Junction and Caernarfon. The intricate scheduling of these routes involved so many depots it was a wonder that vehicles ever found their way home. That they did was down to the expertise of the scheduling offices. During the following months I honed my scheduling skills, which were at their peak demand in advance of the summer period. At quieter times, I was loaned back to the cash office whenever there was a problem.

Evidently, after eighteen months of training I was considered competent enough to relieve the depot superintendent at Blaenau Ffestiniog when he was on holiday. Whilst this seemed a significant accolade, the fact that the depot had no more than a dozen buses and was run single-handedly by the superintendent, with a little help from his sole mechanic, curbed my inflated ego.

You reached Blaenau by a rail journey down the Conwy Valley through the slate mining areas that surround the small town. The famous narrow gauge Ffestiniog railway had been and gone; the tourists were in Porthmadog and the full line had yet to be re-instated between Blaenau and Tan-y-Bwlch. So Blaenau had little to show from its heritage except the Trawsfynydd Reservoir, on its outskirts, that provided water to my homeland in Birmingham and the Black Country.

The small Crosville garage, with only a handful of buses, was actually quite new and it gave me the opportunity to put to good use everything I had learned over the previous eighteen months. It was a pleasant enough job and not very stressful but it could be a little lonely. It was possible to count the cash and complete the administration within the first hour or so of the day. So unless there were any operational problems to address, time could begin to drag from about coffee time. One morning I was sitting quietly when I heard some noises outside the window. It seemed as if something was bumping or rubbing against the wall. I went to the window and found two sides of the depot surrounded by sheep. I knew at that point that there was nothing like the real experience of rural operations to keep ones feet firmly planted on the ground.

My first visit to Wrexham was in 1970. The depot at Wrexham was known for its militancy. The area served many former mining communities and the tribulations of that industry seemed to permeate the culture of all its inhabitants. Wrexham was, however, one of Crosville's larger depots providing a busy local network and main line services between Oswestry and Chester. The union representative in Wrexham was a conductor who knew that the writing was on the wall for his trade so he vehemently resisted any hint of a suggestion of the conversion of services to one-man operation, which was accelerating throughout the industry in the early 'seventies. Vehicles and technology had made the conductor's job superfluous and many routes, particularly in the more rural areas, were being converted to 'omo'. Wrexham depot was determined that it should fight this change to the end and I was sent there in April that year to help revise the schedules that would see the beginning of the end for conductors in that area. Whilst this was an exciting challenge, it also came a month before I was due to get married.

John B Hargreaves, more normally referred to as 'JBH', was probably the most influential individual in the early part of my career. While I was at Crosville he was Traffic Manager and was feared by many for his short fuse temper and intolerance of anything that did not meet his standards. He was a man not to cross but also a man who could be very supportive and loyal to those he believed in. The issue of one-man conversion in Wrexham had become a mission and a matter of principle to the hierarchy of Crosville and drafting in additional resources (like me) to get the schedules prepared for the final assault was an indication of strong intentions.

The local Divisional Manager, Walter Edwards, had lived with the stalemate for some time and was a lot more pragmatic, if not resigned to a drawn out battle. When my newly found scheduling skills arrived at Wrexham, I needed an ally to persuade (confront) JBH that I needed a week off at the end of May to get married. Walter was my ally; battle worn and scarred, another stand-off, albeit with his boss and this time not the Union, was simply in the course of another day's work. The concession was granted with the caveat that, on my return to work I should spend two weeks in Blaenau Ffestiniog. It sounded more like a punishment but was a small price to pay. Wrexham union gradually capitulated, as everyone in Wrexham knew they would eventually, and I was to spend the remainder of my traineeship commuting between Llandudno Junction, Rhyl and Chester learning the 'black art' of engineering and the newly introduced rural subsidies at the Company's Crane Wharf Headquarters in Sealand Road, Chester.

My three years training completed in June 1971, my first deployment was back to Wrexham. Three miles south of Wrexham was a small former tram shed in Johnstown. The depot had lived under the shadow of its bigger neighbour and had, for many years, been under the threat of closure. The small fleet, of about 18 vehicles, had been carefully managed by a small and dedicated staff led by a Clerk-in-Charge, much like Edna's position in Denbigh. My arrival in this position was at first treated sceptically, most convinced that my appearance forebode closure; but after a few weeks the staff, all from a very tightly knit Welsh community, began to warm.

I was now also old enough to start my Public Service Vehicle driving instruction. Coming to terms with the inconsistencies of a crash gearbox and no power steering was novel if not courageous. Being taught to drive double-decks up and down the Welsh foothills was adventurous. When eventually I was deemed ready for my test, I was slightly deflated by the Chester-based driving examiner who concluded that I drove the bus well 'for a car driver'. He passed me, however, and with my treasured PSV licence, I was let loose to try more compliant semi-automatic vehicles which, with power steering, were a lot more comfortable to handle.

The winter of 1971/2 was traumatic for many. The miners were in conflict with Ted Heath's Conservative government and the three day week was upon us. Power cuts were a symptom of the unrest during a bitterly cold period. Early in the new year our newly born son, Daniel, arrived and my spare time was spent with Eddie, my Garage Foreman, collecting bits of coal from the redundant slag heaps that surrounded Johnstown to supplement the meagre fuel allowance we had been allowed by the authorities.

We thought there might be some respite when I was asked to spend two weeks relieving the Depot Superintendent at Dolgellau, who was off sick, only to battle through a snowstorm, with a six-week-old baby, which closed the Horseshoe Pass behind us. But when we arrived at our temporary accommodation in Love Lane into a welcoming, warm and modern flat, we were ready to hibernate in Dolgellau until the trials of the winter had dispersed. Dolgellau was only a small outpost but like so many Crosville garages, generations of the same families had worked there and were loyally protective of their little corner of a greater empire. It was a delight to work in such a family atmosphere, now lost with the closure of so many similar out-stations.

JBH had plans for me. Runcorn was a newly designated development area created to accommodate the housing requirements of an exhausted Merseyside. The depot at Runcorn stood on the side of the canal and was run by a kindly individual, Arthur Waldron, who was due to retire in the summer of 1973. The plan was to create an appointment of Assistant Depot Superintendent that I would be given in preparation for my promotion to Arthur's role. JBH obviously had some difficulty in persuading the Board to create this new post but eventually, in May 1972, I arrived in my first 'real' management post with the grand salary of £1,715 per annum.

Working with Arthur, as I came to learn with a number of my senior colleagues, was the equivalent of a bus industry finishing school. I learnt very quickly that experience, only gained from many years at the helm, was the most valuable qualification you could achieve. I had been thoroughly trained but had zero experience of this vast industry, let alone, life. Arthur was the first of a few highly prized mentors who gave value and depth to being a manager.

Runcorn was in an exciting phase of its development. The Busway, a concept of providing fast, frequent public transport in advance of the housing, at that time was unique to the UK and drew many visitors. Our party piece was to stand in the main centre, at Shopping City, and pronounce the exact arrival of the next bus, which it did without failure, because the Busway track was exclusive to the Crosville services which were protected from any traffic congestion or external disruptions. If there was one blot on this immaculate conception, it was probably the Seddon Pennine buses that were bought to provide the 'T' (for transit) services. They were notoriously unreliable and had a reputation for driving crablike so that you sometimes felt that the backend was likely to overtake the front.

In August 1973 Arthur Waldron retired and I succeeded him with a salary increase of £500 a year. We were planning for a new depot in the New Town and this caused much anticipation. My Divisional Manager and his assistant were Clive Myers and Philip Ayres, two very contrasting characters. Clive enjoyed the drama, often throwing his spectacles across the desk in frustration of any awkward negotiations, which, if nothing more, caused great amusement amongst the Union

Edge Lane depot, Liverpool. The main hub of Crosville's large network of express services to Wales and also to London, was based here and was where I was to undertake training in relation to the planning and charting of the bookings for these services. *(STA)*

A year later, in May 1972, I arrived at Runcorn as Assistant Depot Superintendent, where I was introduced to The Busway. A few years later this Leyland National, which was powered by batteries in a trailer, was used experimentally on The Busway. It was initially delievered to Ribble and is shown here before the Crosville livery was applied. Not only was the busway segregated from other traffic, but in the early days it also appeared to be segregated from the population! This rural looking view belies the fact new town housing was to provide much needed income for Crosville. *(NBC)*

As mentioned in the text, the Seddon Pennine buses were notoriously unreliable. There were, in fact, two batches, 50 with two-door bodies seating 45, some of which were used on the Runcorn Busway. There were also a further 50 dual-purpose vehicles with only a front door. One of the latter is seen above. They came in useful in their later lives, however, when following withdrawal their Gardner engines replaced those in Leyland Nationals *(JS)*

My first appointment after completing three years training was to return to Wrexham and to be put in charge of Johnston depot, a former tram shed some three miles south of the town. This early view shows one of the trams owned by the Western Transport Company, used to open the service. Even in my time at the depot, the redundant tram lines were still visible.

representatives, whilst Phil was cast in the role of peacemaker. The service network developed quickly in Runcorn and with strong inter-urban links to Chester and Liverpool on routes H20–H24, the depot was a good place to be.

This was also the period that saw the introduction of the National Bus Company's flagship bus, the Leyland National. Developed between Leyland and NBC technicians, the National heralded a new era of bus building encouraged by a 50% governmental grant to introduce one-person-operated buses. Like any new bus the National was not without its problems. Runcorn was to be the first Crosville garage to receive the first six and drivers were despatched to Leyland to deliver them to their new home. *En route* two broke down, within the first week two more had collided with each other, a third had argued with a dustcart so that by the end of the first week, we only had one left on the road.

Amazingly, for a sophisticatedly electronic vehicle which engineers, initially, universally loathed, the National was to continue in service for the next 25 years and time has mellowed the sceptics so that it is now looked back upon with some affection. What is true is that the Leyland National was probably the pioneer of our modern day bus and caused the industry to gradually move away from the traditional engineering disciplines to more comprehensive roles with much more electrical expertise.

Runcorn attracted visitors from around the world, mainly civil engineers who wanted to see if the Liverpool overspill with its pioneering bus network really did work. At its centre, Shopping City was still pristine and sparkling when the Queen was invited to officially open the new development. The great and the good were to be gathered to meet Her Majesty and the Duke of Edinburgh and planning meetings to address the visit filled the diary for months in advance of their arrival. It was decided that the Royal party should drive along the Busway to see some of the housing communities and arrive in Shopping City at one of the bus platforms from where they would descend, by escalator, to the shopping area to perform the formalities.

Whilst it was never a concern that Her Majesty would pay any interest in the bus network, Crosville and the officials of the Development Corporation wanted to make sure that Her Royal Highness could see that her point of arrival was the central bus station. It was decided, therefore, to 'discreetly' place a bus at the far end of the platform, well away from where the Royal Party would disembark and where it would cause the least interest. No one had considered Prince Phillip's tendency (notoriety and downright devilment) for deviating from the Royal itinerary.

The great day arrived and officials gathered on the bus platform to welcome the Royal Party. The Queen and Her Escort arrived and were carefully ushered towards the escalator. At the last moment Prince Phillip noticed the bus and swerved in its direction. A look of panic simultaneously spread over every face and Peter Jenner, one of Crosville's head office contingent, raced ahead of the Duke and jumped into the driver's cab of the bus – no doubt in anticipation of preventing the Duke from driving the vehicle away. The Duke climbed on to the platform of the bus to be greeted by a smiling Peter. The Duke glanced down into the driver's cab that was strewn with cigarette butts. He looked Peter in the eye and said "Don't you provide your drivers with ashtrays?" Before waiting for a reply from the dumbstruck Peter, he turned, with a glint in his eye, to return to the waiting Monarch.

I was never to manage the new Runcorn depot. JBH had other plans and in a re-organisation of the Divisions in Cheshire, I was offered another newly created role, this time with the lengthy title of Assistant Divisional Manager, Cheshire North West. The Divisional Manager was Harold Ffoulkes, and we were to be based in the Crane Wharf, the head office of Crosville. Our division had Chester, Ellesmere Port, Runcorn and Warrington depots within it, so I was still on home ground.

Harold, whose career had stretched no further than Chester and Wrexham, felt more comfortable with the more western end of his area. When we were together in the office, our daily ritual at lunchtime was to walk to Chester depot to empty the one-armed bandit. Harold's prized role was Secretary of the Social Club that took precedence over most things. We got on well with our unwritten division of power and I enjoyed a wider scope of planning and re-scheduling services that were now prefaced with 'C' for Chester or 'F' for Mold.

The continuing move towards 100% one-person operation played a big part in my new role. Some of the Liverpool services, like Wrexham, had resisted conversion and, not surprisingly, there was strong opposition in some quarters, particularly at Edge Lane, to the programme. The H5 was a limited stop service running between Warrington and Liverpool Pier Head in just fifty-nine minutes. The H2 was a slower version but observing all stops through Prescot, Whiston and Huyton. The agreed process to negotiate conversions was proceeded by actual real-time checks. The Union nominated an existing one-man operative to drive the bus, in service, and representatives of the management and the union branch would travel on the bus and time its progress, or otherwise.The driver nominated by the Edge Lane Union to undertake the time trial on H2 was known to be the slowest in the depot. The chance of getting from Warrington to Liverpool during the course of a morning, let alone in the seventy minutes allocated, was going to be impossible. However, the nominated driver had other ideas and had obviously decided to rise to the challenge.

We set out in the early morning from Warrington and by the time we had reached Whiston, the trade union representatives were becoming so agitated that one of them could not resist going downstairs to the driver and suggesting, in no uncertain terms, that he slow down. The driver was known not only for his cautious driving but also his quiet manner. He responded in kind by telling his rep, in no uncertain terms, to mind his own business and the journey, by this time with a full peak load, was completed in 68 minutes! The conversion of both routes went ahead.

Hargreaves had moved on to be General Manager of the great Midland Red empire which by now had lost its heartland to the West Midlands Passenger Transport Executive, but functioned like a mint with a hole in the middle through four divisions, based at each corner in Cannock, Leicester, Rugby and Worcester.

At Leicester the Divisional Manager North East was Steve Trennery and he was about to be promoted to Assistant Traffic Manager East based at the company's head office in Edgbaston. It was suggested that I apply for the vacancy and I subsequently came face to face with my 'godfather' once more. The deal was done between Teddy Dravers, now the General Manager at Crosville, and JBH so that my last working day with Crosville would be Leap Day in 1976. The next day I was a Midland Red employee at the grand salary of £4,670 a year and with my first company car!

My eight years in the Crosville family were to prove the most rewarding and educating in my early career. Many years later, I was invited by Clive Myers to speak at a dinner to commemorate the centenary of Crosville, by then in pieces absorbed into the post-deregulation groups. I recalled the spirit of that Company which had evolved from two guys who found running buses more lucrative than building cars!

The Crosville name retained something special for the many people who had come through its ranks on the way to greater things and I concluded my speech with a quote from 'The Sowing and the Harvest' – the first volume of Crosville's colourful history. "There is value in a name. It costs nothing, but people swarm round it like bees round their queen." The Crosville name still has value and its spirit endures.

I gained my conductor's badge (on the left) two weeks after my 18th birthday and my driver's badge three years later. The ones illustrated were replacements issued to me in the East Midlands traffic area.

Chapter 3 – The Midland Red Years

The Leicester divisional office was in Peacock Lane opposite the cathedral. Round the corner was Southgate Street, one of three Leicester depots, the others being Sandacre Street facing St Margaret's Bus Station and the third in South Wigston. The Division was responsible for three additional outlying depots at Hinckley, Coalville and Swadlincote. My only experience of this part of the Midland Red empire had been on one of my 'Day Anywhere' excursions, twelve years earlier, so the learning started on day one. The division had its own schedules office, in which was my first encounter with Tony Depledge, who was later to move on to greater things in Blackpool and as President of the industry's Trade Council and then to meet up with me again when he joined Arriva. Brian Harper, my Area Engineer, had been part of the Harper Brothers business that had been acquired in Hednesford. He was happy in his work that centred around Berni Inns lunches in Churchgate where we would discuss, but not necessarily solve, the problems of the day.

In my role of those who have most supported and influenced me throughout my career, Ted Curtis, my Assistant at Leicester, is the most prominent. Ted had worked for BMMO in Leicester all his life and had no desire to climb any higher than his assistant position. His role had previously been designated Staff Officer, which meant that he handled all staff issues, disciplinary matters and anything else the Divisional Manager off-loaded. He was the most respected man I have ever worked with, at all levels, and his calm, fatherly approach to any problem, rightly earned him a reputation highly esteemed. He and his wife Dot became close family friends who supported both Barbara and I professionally and personally. He had wonderful stories, particularly when conducting in rural Leicestershire, where there was more poultry than passengers on the bus or when he and his driver abandoned their bus in snow drifts in deepest Rutland for the bus only to re-appear several days later. He showed me what patience was, although I was never a good pupil, and what fairness was, as he was rarely criticised on how he handled difficult staff or the most sensitive situations.

Midland Red, although stretched across a huge area of middle England, was still very centrally controlled. The Edgbaston head office was fifty miles from Peacock Lane; the M69 and M6 did not exist so a meeting at head office was a day out on the A47. Whilst the divisions were allowed to suggest service changes, the applications were vetted and processed in Edgbaston. The Divisions were responsible for delivery, in service terms and budgets and for industrial relations that had been very shaky in the early 'seventies. As a result, Midland Red had recognised the need for full time trade union representatives, one of whom, Cyril Paragreen, was based at Southgate Street. Cyril was paid as a driver but in my five years in Leicester, I never saw him in uniform. To the outside, he looked like one of the management and to some degree had as much, if not more, influence.

I was still very naïve and a little arrogant about trade unions, as other than at Wrexham, I had not really been exposed to militancy. The apparent trade union power in Midland Red took some getting used to. When drivers' hours regulations were revised in 1970, the trade union had persuaded the Midland Red management that one way to solve the acute driver shortage was for the basic week to be Monday to Friday and for all weekend work to be voluntary overtime. The Union were so keen on this proposal that they offered to take responsibility for driver coverage at the weekend. In reality, it never happened and it took many years to re-instate the acceptance that this business was a seven-day-week affair and drivers should be prepared to be scheduled on any day of the week.

Negotiations with Cyril could be a turbulent event. In truth, his experience and cunning far outmanoeuvred mine and there were times when he delighted in playing with me like a cat with a mouse. On one occasion, the negotiations of a set of scheduling changes to which the Union were vehemently opposed, had ground on for some hours. I was determined to keep the reps there all night if it achieved the desired outcome but by 9pm Cyril had had enough and, with a dramatic gesture, stormed out leaving me and the local Depot Superintendent staring at each other, without a clue what to do next. After an uncomfortable twenty minutes or so, Cyril and his entourage returned and a solution was found. The next day he came to see me on his own. "I had you worried there, didn't I", he said. He knew he held the cards and he knew I had nowhere to go but our relationship balanced out from then on and, for all his posturing, we worked better together after that episode.

The relationship between BMMO and Leicester City Transport (LCT) was legendary and incredible. A system of black Area Stop Signs prevented Midland Red, or any other operator, from setting down any passenger between the City Centre and the stop sign on outward journeys and from picking up along the same corridor on inward journeys, thus protecting the municipal operator from any semblance of competition. The relationship between the two operators had been so acrimonious over the years that even when the Country was united in the war effort, BMMO and LCT were battling it out in Traffic Court in 1942.

The General Managers of council-controlled bus companies were all-powerful. Whilst their dedication was to the 'Mayor and Corporation', a successful General Manager was able to use his knowledge and political skills to blind his employers and establish his dominance. The finest example of this was Geoffrey Graham Hilditch, a Lancastrian who had spent his earlier managementship in Yorkshire but was now well established in the power room of LCT. An engineer by trade, vehicle suppliers courted him and politicians were in awe of him. He was small in stature, magnified by his huge office where you found him standing, rarely seated, at the head of a conference table that filled the office.

He never missed an opportunity to assert his presence and authority. On one occasion, I had dared to operate a school bus that was considered to be in LCT 'territory'. The immediate result was a summons of the senior operating personnel from Edgbaston to Abbey Park Road, the head office of LCT. Robin Jones, the Midland Red Traffic Manager, Geoff Marchant, his Chief Assistant and I duly arrived one afternoon to be allowed into the great hall in descending order of importance. So after 45 minutes sat in the corridor, as if I was waiting to be summoned into the Headmaster's study for a caning, I was finally called in to join the cross-examination. To this day I do not understand why the might of Midland Red allowed itself to be humiliated in this way but that aura that surrounded Hilditch was capable of spinning over his adversaries, of which there were many.

The decline of the industry had accelerated throughout the 'sixties which proved to be an affluent era when anyone with any money bought a car. Hargreaves and those around him realised that more inventive ways of stemming this decline needed to be found, and the industry's first real experience of the art of consultancy made its entrance.

The Market Analysis Project (MAP) was well intentioned. Researchers would track passenger movements and demand and try to align service provision to those figures. To be fair, many of the routes had remained unchanged for decades and the time had come to think radically about the resources we were using. Unfortunately, thinking radically can sometimes be a step too far. The resultant new networks were often unworkable and I don't think we ever anticipated our customers' revolt against change.

Each network had been carefully marketed with new local identities allegedly representing some tenuous link to the community it served. Names such as 'Tellus', 'Hotspur' and 'Lancer' suddenly entered our vocabulary although the people that mattered, the passengers, seemed totally unimpressed and not a little confused. MAP was succeeded by VNP (Viable Network Project) that sought to put right some of the fundamental wrongs of its predecessor but the concept had already lost its credibility. There was recognition, however, that we had a product to market and, if the industry was to survive, we had to sell it like any other consumer product. A new brand of busman was born – the marketeer.

Divisional and Senior Managers were invited with their wives (I cannot remember any senior female personnel at that time) to the Company's annual black tie dinner in a hotel at Edgbaston. The event, whilst formal, was an opportunity to meet those in the organisation you might not come across from one year end to the next. One of the highlights, if you were not the individual tasked with delivering, was the after dinner speech. Unfortunately, this was usually awarded to a newcomer and with a little more than six months in my new position, the task fell to me. I was terrified; Brian Harper was dismissive, assuring me that most of my colleagues would be 'too far gone' to remember anything I said. I saw it as another Herculean task set by my mentor JBH. On the night in question I could hardly eat let alone drink and, when I was called upon to perform, I was almost shaking. The night was saved by my dialogue denouncing VNP as a cover for a pornographic ring called 'Very Naughty Postcards'. I suggested that its financial projections were actually cricket scores that JBH (a keen cricketer) was yet to attain. If I was going down, I was going down fighting. On realising my audience was fully absorbed, I completed my performance by asking the whole gathering to rise and toast Liverpool Football Club's latest European triumph. I survived the evening and created a little folklore.

Whilst most of my northeast division centred on Leicestershire, Swadlincote depot ventured locally into Staffordshire and Derbyshire and into Derby on the X12 to and from Birmingham. My first visit to Swadlincote was on a very grey and dull April morning as drizzle developed into a full rainstorm. The long descent from Woodville into Swadlincote was my imagined picture of entering the bowels of hell. The area was spotted with slag heaps, the enduring signs of the final decline of the coal industry in this area, and whilst attempts were eventually made to improve its outlook – one of the slag heaps became a ski slope – Swadlincote on a dull

The management gathering at Midland Red in the late 1970s. My trusted Assistant Ted Curtis on the left, the Company's Chief Engineer Robin Westbrook and Chief Assistant Traffic Manager Geoff Marchant, me and the Company Secretary and my area Engineer.

The Sandacre Street depot at Leicester was very close to St Margaret's bus station. Inside the depot, with a D9 to its left, is a Plaxton-bodied Leyland Leopard which was classified as LC11 by Midland Red

When BMMO ceased to build double-deckers they ordered Alexander-bodied Daimler Fleetlines. No. 6165, new in 1969, is shown in St Margaret's bus station, which was the focal point and terminus of Midland Red's services in Leicester.

Also in St Margaret's Bus Station is No. 5922, an S23 with BMMO chassis and body, which had been delivered in 1969 and was withdrawn in 1980.

rainy day would never be inviting. My dealings with Staffordshire County Council brought me into contact with a young local government officer called Julian Peddle.

Towards the end of my first spell in Leicester my colleague and neighbouring Divisional Manager, Arthur Townsend, was promoted to ATM East, to replace Steve Trennery, who had departed to Maidstone. It was decided that I had coped easily with six depots so adding four more would not be too onerous. So I inherited Rugby, Leamington, Nuneaton and Stratford on Avon that meant more travelling into the far reaches of Warwickshire. My 'Day Anywhere' escapades were coming home to haunt me.

After three years I was expected to move on and encouraged to apply for Assistant Traffic Manager roles. An application to join Ribble Motor Services in Preston resulted in an enlightening interview with the then General Manager, Fred Dark, who notoriously rarely worked after lunch, and my first meeting with his then Traffic Manager, Brian King. Further interviews at Hants and Dorset and South Wales Transport in Swansea followed. This last interview went well and I was to be offered the post but JBH stepped in; he had other ideas for me.

Privatisation was looming, the days of the National Bus Company were numbered and senior personnel were preparing for a revolution that would make many millionaires and see some disappear forever. Midland Red was to become four separate stand-alone units in readiness for sale and Midland Red East was to revert to my original division. Each unit was to have its own 'head office structure', a General Manager, Traffic Manager and Finance man and, in advance of their probable sale, the home team would have a distinct advantage and inside track when bidding began. JBH assured me that a position was secured for me within this new structure and that, in the least, I would be Traffic Manager. This was not what I wanted to hear. I had been Divisional Manager for five years and had become more independent and distanced from Edgbaston. I did not relish facing the prospect of being relegated to number two with an outsider being brought in above me as General Manager. I made my views known but was cautioned with patience.

At Leicester City Transport, the Deputy General Manager, Peter Goodrich, was due to retire and out of the blue Hilditch rang me and suggested an application from me, which he said, with his support, would be looked on favourably by the City's Transport Committee. Looking back, I was too easily coerced into selling my soul. JBH was advocating 'wait and see' whilst Hilditch was tempting me with a 60% increase in salary. Would I have become an NBC millionaire? We will never know.

My competitors for the LCT job, including Tony Depledge, were gathered together for a pre-interview dinner. They were convinced to a man that the job was mine. Ironically, on April 1st 1981, I was interviewed by a semi-circle of eleven councillors and officers of Leicester City Council. Within twenty-four hours I received a personal visit at Peacock Lane by Hilditch who offered me the position as his Deputy. With the benefit of hindsight, I can indulge myself in regret but the experience of the following four years, however unpleasant at times, taught me that my chosen career was not always going to be perfect.

I had to inform Hargreaves of my decision to accept Hilditch's offer. Not surprisingly, he was furious, threatened to use that evening's Long Service Awards presentations at the Botanic Gardens in Aston to expose me (which in the event he never did) and had difficulty in speaking to me during my three months notice that he insisted I should fulfil to the day, despite Hilditch pleading for my early release. There is little doubt that Hilditch had pulled off a coup. Regardless of what he thought of my abilities, he had prised a rising star away from his arch rival and NBC defections to municipalities were virtually unheard of. My salary rose overnight from £8,000 to £14,000 with a generous car allowance and I took my place in Abbey Park Road.

This scene in Shrewsbury shows No. 5157, a 1962 Leyland Leopard with bodywork by Weymann, which had the BMMO classification LS18 It is about to depart for Hereford via Ludlow. Although BMMO was still building vehicles, more were needed, hence the order for 100 Leopards, 25 of which had Weymann bodies and the balance were bodied by Willowbrook. *(AEJ)*

Whereas Midland Red had its own manufacturing arm, Leicester's collaboration with Dennis resulted in large numbers of Dominators being found in the LCT fleet. By far and away the majority of them were bodied by East Lancs. *(DC)*

The fleet also included MCW Metrobuses, another of the new generation of double-deckers emerging during the early 1980s. *(BB)*

Chapter 4 – The Leicester City Transport Years

My sentence started at the beginning of July 1981; the first four years were coloured by disappointment, frustration and distrust; the second four years were to start with satisfaction and end in tears. I was under no illusion that Hilditch would be a difficult man to work with. My motivation from the start was, if I survived, that I would replace him when he retired or moved on to something else. He controlled everything. In one of our rare moments of confrontation I asked him why he wanted a Deputy when he wanted to do everything himself. He ignored my question as he did with everything he did not consider important.

There were some good people at LCT. The schedules department was run by Les Warneford who was to become Stagecoach's UK Managing Director and who, to this day, insists I swindled him out of two weeks holiday when he left to go to Grimsby. David Kent was LCT's long suffering Chief Engineer and Bill Bishop who replaced John Chadwick when he moved to the south coast, was Traffic Superintendent.

It was a well-run department. Service levels were attractive and, run by an engineer, vehicle standards were also good. One could not help but admire Hilditch's ability to manipulate his political masters who were ignorant of the most rudimentary rules of business. One Transport Committee was dominated by one councillor's objection to a bus stop site. After a lengthy debate the tiring chairman moved on to any other business during which the department's entire vehicle purchases for the following year were approved on the nod.

The Leicester City network, whilst comprehensive, had one quirk. Because most services were linked across the city centre, thus avoiding a terminal loop, the inbound route number was never the same as the outbound; so that if the 29 route to Stoneygate was linked to the 54 route to Stocking Farm the inbound journeys from Stoneygate to the City Centre would show 54 and similarly the inbound journeys from Stocking Farm to the City Centre would show 29.

It was also the days of the Bell Punch machine that had five barrels of pre-printed and pre-valued tickets that, as fares denominations grew, meant more ingenious combinations of tickets to total the required fare. This nightmare was finally resolved by the introduction of the first Wayfarer machines (Wayfarer 1) that, during their initial period of their development, had some drivers longing for the return of the Bell Punch.

Hilditch was obviously heavily occupied in the selection and purchase of buses and his collaboration with Dennis meant that the fleet during the 'eighties was almost entirely dominated by Dominators. At over two hundred vehicles the majority of the fleet were double-decks, but the Department was also blessed with its first Dennis single-decks, the Falcon. Whilst the Dennis vehicles survived a short generation, they were never a popular vehicle and soon disappeared.

Hilditch was ambitious and expansionist. The Corporation boundaries were seen not as a constraint but more an opportunity to stretch. In May 1983, the 'Maidstone Flyer' took this to the extreme. Our colleague municipal operators at Burnley and Pendle Transport had decided to introduce a regular express service, aimed at day-trippers, between their area and London. Their logo, inspired by the Witches of Pendle, was a witch on a broomstick, giving rise to the route's name 'The Burnley and Pendle Flyer'. On a modest scale this was relatively successful but drivers' hours regulations meant that the return trip could not be completed by a single driver and a midway point, that could provide driver reliefs, was needed.

The route was diverted through Leicester and LCT began its involvement in express travel. It was not long before all parties were persuaded that there was a market northbound from London as well as day traffic southbound. To provide earlier journeys northbound from London would require a southern-based operator, so Maidstone Corporation were canvassed and joined the rapidly expanding venture. If you were running coaches to Maidstone, why stop there? The lure of Dover and links to the cross-channel ferries was irresistible. And the fairly modest day trip from Burnley to the capital had ballooned into a daily (and fairly complicated) timetable between Lancashire and the south coast. Whilst cross-city operation in Leicester was manageable, cross London operation was another thing altogether. It was not long before major delays and vehicle breakdowns far from home became unsustainable. Our highly sceptical colleagues elsewhere in the municipal sector were eventually rewarded with a smirk of 'I told you so' and the 'Maidstone Flyer' flew no more. The cost of this grand failure had been astronomical but Hilditch had somehow managed to keep the politicians at bay.

Most of the family bus operating businesses in Leicestershire had long since been swallowed up by the great BMMO. One, however, had retained its long held independence. Gibson Brothers of Barlestone had proved that a simple service with loyal local support was the key to success. It operated hourly on the hour from both ends of the route between Leicester and Market Bosworth. The intermediate villages of Desford and Newbold Verdun meant that the service was not simply reliant on patronage to and from the nearby City but enjoyed many local point-to-point journeys. It therefore came as a little surprise when Hilditch announced that LCT was going to acquire Gibsons. Midland Red had been known to be courting the Gibson owners for years so selling to LCT was not going to be without controversy and was certainly a coup for Hilditch who was probably more motivated by stealing the march on his NBC adversaries than running buses in rural Leicestershire.

Midland Red had gone through its re-organisation; Midland Red East, soon to be re-branded Midland Fox, was now headed by Peter Lutman, with Trevor Petty as his Traffic Manager and a newcomer to the industry, David Martin, as his Finance Manager. Deregulation was looming but the 'Fox' management was impatient.

The constraints of the Area Stop Signs, the 440 yard protective condition placed on Midland Red's predecessors by the 1930 Traffic Act, had been a thorn in that Company's side for over fifty years. Previous attempts to remove the restrictions had come to nought. An earlier BMMO Traffic Manager, OC Power, had offered to pay the entire profits from lifting the restriction to the City of Leicester, but had been denied the opportunity. In 1984 Midland Fox decided their time had come, with deregulation on the horizon, to once and for all challenge their enforced exclusion from running local services within the boundaries of the City of Leicester. Despite the inevitability of the outcome, Leicester City Council, with Hilditch leading the charge, mounted its opposition. But the publication of the Government's White Paper 'Buses', foretelling a new era, seemed to nullify the proceedings and Midland Fox was successful in removing the barrier that had kept them, and their illustrious predecessors, at bay for more than fifty years. This was the green light they had wished for and they pressed ahead, encouraged in the background by their now Regional Director, soon to become Chairman, John Hargreaves.

In July 1984, the introduction of the 'Fox Cub', a fleet of 16-seater Ford Transit minibuses was to challenge the supremacy and monopoly of LCT and the municipality was stunned. Midland Fox heralded its innovation by claiming the move would offer 30% more journeys to the travelling public of Leicester. Hilditch was not going down without a fight and looked to me, with my knowledge of my former employer to produce counter challenges that would take the war to Midland Fox. Hilditch wanted LCT vehicles on every Fox route in central Leicestershire; I was reluctant and was more keen to ensure that our core business was protected firstly and where possible seek some compromise with Fox who were coming at us with a low-cost operation we were unlikely to be able to match. It was also becoming plain that the City Council's politicians were becoming uncomfortable with the thought of a full scale competitive war in Leicester which, to some, was too close to the philosophy of the 1985 Transport Act which they vehemently opposed.

In his arrogance for the fight, Hilditch could not see the internal opposition that was building against his strategy and whilst the Transport Committee's Chairman, Henry Dunphy, remained loyal to Hilditch for as long as he believed his political career could manage, it was clear that Hilditch had to back off or risk isolation, whch resulted in his final downfall. I was an easy target for his wrath but in truth did not have the influence with which he credited me. The Leader of the Council and the ruling Labour Party, Peter Soulsby, did talk to me about the impact that Fox could have and I did suggest caution. LCT had much more to lose in a prolonged and costly fight and Midland Fox, with the corridor restrictions now lifted, was capturing hundreds of former LCT passengers without any additional cost whatsoever. Where once their inter-urban services had been legally compelled to pass bus stops without stopping, they now had the freedom to 'poach' quite legitimately.

Soulsby accepted my counsel and Hilditch's departure was inevitable. He bore his rejection badly and carried his conviction, that I had single-handedly engineered his downfall, for years thereafter. His return to LCT some years later was to a council-owned company that had moved on from the days of the municipal warlord and was on the verge of being sold into that privatisation so despised by his political masters of the early 'eighties.

Whilst the normal Council channels took their own time to process his replacement, in due course I was appointed Director of the now re-named Leicester CityBus. I took my place amongst the senior officers of the Council and at the head of an organisation that was politically braced for the impact of the 1985 Transport Act but in truth was already suffering from the financial impact of the free market. I received a letter from Hilditch's predecessor, Lesley Smith, who had been General Manager from 1966 to 1975. His warm congratulations were to have a prophetic undertone as he reminded me that I was now a member of an exclusive group of eight who had managed Leicester's bus company since its inception in 1901, four of whom were still alive. I did not realise at that time that my name was to be the last on that particular role of honour although one would appear for a second time.

There was an irony in the campaign that the municipal sector launched against the Bus Bill. Within a few years of the introduction of deregulation on 26th October 1986, many of the municipal operations had succumbed to sale or, in a few sad cases, had given up the fight and disappeared forever. Some stalwarts have doggedly resisted selling up but they represent a shadow of the pre and post war years when municipal transport was at its peak and was, I believe, the envy of many in the nationalised sector.

My early years in charge of LCB were dominated by the political anti-deregulation campaign and the more significant challenge of living in the newly competitive world that the Council's Transport Department had, for so long, monopolised. The Department was quietly re-structured to become an 'arms length' council-owned company. The Board, chaired by Peter Soulsby, was still populated by politicians but with more legal interest from the Council's City Attorney. Meetings with Midland Fox slowly became more cordial and attempts were made to find some compromise to the over-bussing that their minibus revolution had created. Their original grandiose plans had been stalled by difficulties in recruitment; the wages for minibus driving were not attractive. The full-sized Fox conventional services continued into the historical Midland Red strongholds such as Thurnby Lodge alongside their Cubs, but that duplication was costly so that neither side was feeling any benefit from the vastly increased service levels.

The Midland Fox management were, by now, becoming distracted by the prospects of privatisation and it became clear very quickly, that their company would not feature in the initial dash to acquire the more lucrative former NBC subsidiaries. In 1987 I produced a comprehensive plan to submit to Leicester City Council that LCB should attempt a bid for Midland Fox. Our letter to the Secretary of State urging him to put pressure on NBC to consider a bid from the municipality was met with a fairly bland reply, which suggested such a move might not be in the interests of free competition. The sale of Midland Fox, therefore, struggled on without a municipal bid and only came to some conclusion when supported by a 30% stake from Stevensons of Uttoxeter, headed by its rising star, Julian Peddle.

In the meantime, LCB would have to generate new business from somewhere now that Midland Fox had established its business in our heartland. It was also clear that there was little point in throwing resources against Fox's inter-urban routes that generally had the advantage of their outlying depots and a lower cost base than their expensive, council-owned, neighbour. Loughborough, just twelve miles away, looked like an opportunity. Trent ran local services in the town but these had been neglected. Despite their image nowadays, immediately post deregulation, like many of their former NBC colleagues who had suddenly become business magnates, Trent were not keen to invest or spend any money that did not have a short term payback.

We devised a plan to do in Loughborough what Fox had done to us in Leicester – operate a series of minibus routes in and around the town which, we were convinced, would quickly encourage Trent to abandon its outstation and retrench to the safety of Derbyshire. We wanted the image of this network to be different to our operations in Leicester; in fact we wanted to play down the council ownership of our venture in this Conservative heartland of Leicestershire. We adopted a very environmental green and yellow livery and opted for the recently introduced Optare buses. For a brand name we wanted to use the highly popular JRR Tolkien books and call our buses 'Hobbits'. We were quickly advised that there might be trademark implications so approached the Tolkien estate for permission to use the name. Unbeknown to us and presumably to most of the literary world, the rights of the Tolkien books had been sold by JRR's family to the Saul Zaentz Company, Film Producers in Berkeley, California. A series of faxes and international telephone calls, as the launch date drew near, frustratingly failed to resolve the Americans intransigence, or lack of understanding why a minor English bus company should want to tarnish the Tolkien legacy by painting the name 'Hobbit' on the side of their buses.

In the end time ran out and we had to quickly find a replacement name. So it was that the 'Trippits' appeared on the streets of Loughborough and Leicester CityBus's first real competitive venture outside the comfort of its home began.

There was a great deal of excitement amongst those LCB personnel deployed to recruit and launch the new business. Trent immediately retaliated by registering competition on two Leicester routes but our experience with Fox had hardened us to attacks and there was a determination to make Loughborough Coach and Bus (note LCB!) work. On 10th July 1987 the 'Trippits' were introduced to the residents of Loughborough and within eleven months we were celebrating our millionth passenger. The only problem was that Trent had not gone away as we had hoped and in consequence the new venture was struggling to make money.

The Managing Director of Trent, who had led their management buy-out, was Brian King. I think Brian was born wily and he realised he could get more than money out of the situation in Loughborough. We met and he was prepared to sell but his price was high. He wanted cash for the property, the Trent depot in The Rushes, but a stake in Leicester CityBus for his business. Financially this might have been attractive but politically it was impossible to see the LCB shareholders, Leicester City Council, conceding any party of their equity. Discussions rumbled on for some months and with my support a deal was eventually struck in which Trent would acquire 5% of the council's company. Needless to say there were a number of councillors who were less than comfortable with this part (however small) privatisation.

The years immediately post deregulation were difficult for council-owned companies whose financial freedom had been deliberately restricted by the government in the hope that the undertakings would be quickly sold into the private sector and local authority control, often by Labour, would quickly diminish. LCB's problems had been exacerbated by the Traffic Commissioner's decision to give Midland Fox the freedom of the city and, it has to be said, its own inability through union agreements and council reluctance, to seek new markets.

LCB's engineering department continued to undertake much of the council's maintenance work under licence but even that was difficult to make profitable. In fact the whole idea of profit was alien to the Labour administration that was still smarting over the Act that had deprived them of overall control. At the time of the opposition to the Bus Bill and the consequent Act, I had strong feelings that 'public transport' was just that – better controlled by the public sector that would consider passenger interests and public service before profits.

Dennis Dominator No. 68 is seen here operating on the former Gibson Brothers of Barlestone service to Market Bosworth. The acquisition of this business and the branching out into Leicestershire had caused some surprise at the time. *(DC)*

Leicester had a small coach fleet and when Burnley and Pendle Transport commenced their 'Flyer' service it was not long before these vehicles became involved into what became a Burnley to Dover service. It seemed obvious to me that such an operation was unsustainable and so it proved to be. *(JH)*

The introduction of 'Fox Cubs' by Midland Red was a significant threat to Leicester City Transport, and a line of the competitors is seen here in the centre of the city. *(JH)*

The management team at Leicester CityBus (l to r) Bill Bishop (Operations Director), David Kent (Chief Engineer), me, Tony Wills (Finance Director) and Roger Merry-Howe (Company Secretary).

Once the die had been cast, there was little point in continuing this resistance and a more pragmatic approach should have been more sensible. But many opposing politicians could not bring themselves to accept that things had moved on and, whilst the companies were legally at 'arms-length', councillors were often reluctant to take the responsibilities of Directors and serve on the bus company's board preferring instead to meddle from the Council sidelines. There were, inevitably, many councillors in the background who did not understand, or chose to ignore, what shadow directors really were.

The Council were not eager to re-negotiate the engineering contract which was becoming onerous, Loughborough Coach and Bus, despite our efforts to build on a successful start by expanding further into rural Leicestershire, was still losing money and the core business in central Leicester was suffering from real competition from anyone who cared to try their hand. We knew that we needed some radical changes to the structure of the company, particularly its cost base and its fares policy, so the Executive Directors drew together an action plan that we believed would address the challenges.

Not surprisingly, there was strong union resistance to anything that looked like redundancy and it was not difficult for the union representatives to solicit support from willing councillors who did not have any directorial responsibilities on the bus company's board. Too many issues were being discussed in 'smoke-filled rooms' and not at board level and the management was experiencing more opposition from a union that had the confidence of political support. A series of strikes disrupted the attempts to make changes and although the Council leadership was outwardly showing support to the management's efforts, it was clear that this support was not robust enough to last long.

The management realised that the company would at best stagnate, at worst collapse, if it could not achieve the privatised freedoms its competitors were now enjoying. So in June 1988 it sought permission from the company's board to put together a management bid for the undertaking and, surprisingly, permission was granted. By autumn we had launched our buy-out exhibition and set about persuading our employees where their future lay. The trade union had other ideas and made it clear that a Workers Co-operative was the model that they preferred. So we were on parallel courses but soon to collide.

The thirty-nine point action plan involved many issues, including wage cuts and redundancies, which were going to be difficult for a trade union in a council-owned company to accept. Although they had experienced first hand how deregulation was affecting the industry, there was a public reluctance to join the new world. The fact that the Directors were advocating a management led buy-out was treated with suspicion, scepticism and outright hostility.

In the midst of all this it was agreed that I should speak to Peter Lutman, my opposite number at Midland Fox, about the disposal of the Loughborough business. The New Year of 1989 brought no respite and certainly no reduction in the opposition to the action plan and the buy-out proposals. At a meeting of all twenty-three union representatives to discuss the way ahead, my presentation was met with silence. After a short recess, the full-time T&GWU officer, Derek Whale, read from a prepared statement that the unions were not prepared to enter into any

The new arms-length Leicester company initially applied the new fleetname to the existing livery, as on this Dennis Dominator which has bodywork by Marshall. *(DC)*

However, before long a new livery entirely utilising grey, red and white was introduced. *(DC)*

negotiations with the present management structure. The meeting broke up and Whale came back into the room to tell me that he had been 'hi-jacked' before the meeting and that a letter had gone to some of the councillors from a few of the representatives demanding my dismissal. This was not a great surprise as I had heard similar rumours.

I arranged to see the recently appointed chair of the board, Councillor Maggie Stagg, who had rather had the post forced upon her, as others amongst her colleagues had distanced themselves. I told her forthrightly that the Board either had to back me or sack me but it could not be a decision for a few, heavily influenced councillors who were not directly involved in the running of the company. She was adamant that the issues were a matter between the management and the union and that she had relayed this view to her colleagues. I was not convinced; there was a leadership battle in the Council and this was easy ammunition for the pretenders.

Towards the end of January another full union meeting was held in the hope of advancing the action plan but a longer recess this time resulted in a more detailed response from the representatives who stated that they would not negotiate whilst I remained Managing Director. Interestingly, the AUEW full time official Bridget Paton, who had always been sympathetic to me, and supported the management's intentions, asked if the Council *could* sack me. I told her it had to be the Board who would have to call an extraordinary general meeting to do so. In any event, my dismissal would not change the figures, if anything it would only worsen the position by delaying the inevitable actions needed for recovery.

There was also some discord amongst the other executive directors. The Finance Director, Tony Wills had joined the company from outside the industry. There were suggestions that he was having clandestine talks with some of the more militant union officers including the branch secretary Phil Hardy, an idealist left-winger whose political ambitions were evident for all to see. Whilst there was obviously a lack of cohesion between the unions and particularly a discomfort amongst the full time officials, Hardy felt that the winds were with him and his contacts in the political circles of the Council were encouraging his defiance with promises of a change in regime and policy.

There were also strong rumours that a report had been produced for the senior members of the Council about the future of LCB and its management structure. None of the executive directors had seen it or had had any input into it. Some of the union reps were tiring of the hostilities and the fact that no progress was being made. A suggestion that a different approach to privatisation might heal some wounds was broached; an ESOP (Employee Share Option Plan) might be an acceptable compromise. It was agreed that this was an option worth exploring but, at a time when there were so many different factions jockeying for control, it was unlikely that any consensus could be reached. Arrangements were put in place for the steering group of the Workers Co-operative to meet the management and see if we could find common ground for an ESOP. The meeting was set for Friday 10th February but never happened.

Late on the afternoon of Tuesday 7th February, I received an unexpected visit from the Chief Executive of the Council, Derek Mellor. Derek had always been supportive and we had always had a good working relationship from the days I had been with Midland Red when he had been the City's Attorney. His opening line was that he had "bad news" and I knew the end was beginning. Leicester City Council was never slow in sacking chief officers; there had been a steady stream of political dismissals during the years that the Council had been Labour controlled. He told me that I would be summoned to a meeting with the City Attorney and Councillor Stagg the following day when my parting would be discussed. There had been an executive meeting in the Council the previous evening that had decided that they no longer had confidence in me and that I had to go.

Derek thought the whole thing "naïve and distasteful" but, in truth, he had seen this process so many times before, he was somewhat hardened, although he didn't show it. We talked about the future of the company; he had advised the Leadership that my dismissal could bring greater pressures from our creditors. I asked him who would replace me and was told that Tony Wills would not be given the job, but would assume control until a replacement could be found. He advised me to get some legal advice and left me after two hours more distraught than I was. When he had gone it suddenly hit me that I was about to be unemployed for the first time in my life.

Success in my career had brought some degree of comfort and stability. In the very early days of my marriage, when we had first lived in a small one up, one down terrace in Llysfaen above Colwyn Bay, Barbara and I had struggled to make ends meet. My promotions had gradually given us a lifestyle we had never envisaged at the start. My move from Midland Red to Leicester City had helped us take on a larger mortgage to buy a bigger house and to pay for my son's education. Now, in the course of one conversation, all this looked under threat and I was not certain that I would be able to cope with the imposed changes and challenges that we were about to face.

It is at times like these that you value the person closest to you. When I got home that evening, fully dejected and totally self-absorbed, Barbara, after her initial outburst of indignant anger, took control. We sat and discussed how we could afford to complete our son's schooling by selling our house and moving into a terrace near to the school. We pondered the options for me to find work and what we could sell to raise money. In a few hours my wife had pulled me away from my self-centred despair. While I was losing a job, I realised my family stood to lose a great deal more. I rang a known employment advisor who suggested a local company who would handle my case and then, at Barbara's insistence and with great reluctance, I phoned John Hargreaves.

The following days took on their own life. There were daily meetings with my lawyer who became the go-between and an astute negotiator with the Council and, surreally, I continued to manage the business although I was not allowed to attend the Board meeting that eventually cemented my destiny. My fellow directors were understandably uneasy with what was going on around them. The Council had decided to bring consultants in to appraise the company and the action plans yet I was allowed to continue discussions with Lutman and we reached an agreement on the sale of Loughborough Coach and Bus. The Leader of the Conservative opposition party wanted to see me as he obviously sensed some political advantage but I declined – now was not the time to fuel political ambition.

Inevitably, the negotiations on my settlement became protracted although the Council's insistence that I resign (rather than be sacked) was a little bizarre. In the end my resignation was submitted to an Extraordinary Meeting on 2nd March and my package, which included a glowing reference from the Leader of the Council, later to be Sir Peter Soulsby, was agreed. My 'integrity, commitment and conscientiousness', had seemingly not been sufficient to warrant supporting me any longer.

The following day, my last day in the employment of a council-owned company, I met staff and union officials for the final time. Slightly touchingly, many of my union adversaries were more than contrite and I think for the first time realised that, achieving the removal of the Managing Director did not change their position or solve any of their problems. What they didn't know was, that far from despatching me to the ranks of the unemployed, I had started my new position two days earlier.

One of the large fleet of Dennis Dominators operated by Leicester is shown outside Leicester station. This particular vehicle was one of three exchanged before delivery with South Yorkshire PTE for three Dennis Dorchester coaches. The body, although built to Alexander's design, was actually constructed by East Lancs. *(DC)*

Chapter 5 – The Derby City Transport Years

My telephone call to John Hargreaves had been difficult to make. He had never really forgiven me for my defection and I fully expected a short response. In the event, he made it much easier than I deserved to expect but, as usual with JBH, he saw an opportunity. In his post-deregulation portfolio, he was Chairman of Luton and District. L&D had been one of the later ex-NBC companies to enter the privatised world and had done so by being the first employee-led buy-out. The employees had been led by a former supervisor, Graham Cummings. He had assumed the mantle of Managing Director as if it had been made for him. He was a jovial guy who was never far from his roots and whilst not the most experienced in management, his relationship with his workforce had persuaded them to invest their savings into acquiring L&D.

Having succeeded with one, Graham and JBH were on the lookout for further opportunities usually where a management buy-out was unlikely to succeed. Two of the Scottish units, Clydeside and Western were still to be sold and the employee option was likely to be preferred. JBH thought I could work on this bid as Managing Director designate and if it failed he would guarantee me twelve months salary. We had agreed to meet a few days later to discuss this in more detail but, by the time we met, a further option had emerged. Derby City Council had decided to sell their transport undertaking and the employees had approached Luton for advice and support. Given my previous experience, this would be a more appropriate venture for me to lead and on which I could work from the outset. It would be a highly competitive sale.

The management under the incumbent Managing Director, Peter Crook, were known to want to lead an MBO and there would be interest from other ex-NBC buy-outs, like neighbouring Trent, as this would be one of the first municipal undertakings to voluntarily opt for privatisation. It was agreed that I should meet the employee buy-out committee led by the trade union branch secretary Iain Wordsworth and branch chairman John Tidbury. The irony of this was there for all to see but I actually felt more comfortable with the backing of former NBC colleagues and relished the opportunity to make this succeed. I knew the rumours of my impending departure from CityBus were already circulating, although at that stage nothing had been announced officially, so I was faced with admitting openly to these trade union reps what had happened in LCB so no one was under any illusion about their new leader. Their encouragement was refreshing and the story they related to me was certainly compelling.

On 16th February 1989, three bus drivers had arrived at the Regional Headquarters of the National Westminster Bank in Nottingham hoping to make a little piece of history. The Banking Executive they met that day freely admitted later that he had expected the interview to last twenty minutes and that would be that. In fact, by the end of the meeting he was so impressed by the drivers' enthusiasm and support that he agreed to assist them, provided that they found proper legal and financial advice and, most importantly, they recruited a competent management team.

To understand why this meeting took place at all, we need to turn the clock back several months, to events that were to lead to the privatisation of Derby City Transport. DCT had been a municipal bus operator since 1899 and, in common

A large number of Daimler Fleetlines had been in the Derby fleet when Leyland announced its discontinuance, so several different chassis were then tried to find a successor. A solitary Metrobus had been taken into stock in 1980 as No. 102 (GRA 102V). *(DC)*

As part of Derby's campaign against the Transport Bill in 1985, one of the Fleetlines was painted in this striking livery to emphasise the council's concerns. *(DC)*

The Derby City Transport Employees buy-out committee.

The new Managing Director of Derby City Transport Limited.

with all Council-owned transport departments, had been re-structured into an arms-length, but still 100% council-owned company, following the 1985 Transport Act. Unlike the enforced sales of the National Bus Company subsidiaries, there had been no rush to fully privatise the ex-municipalities and only adverse financial circumstances had resulted in two or three of the smaller undertakings falling unwillingly into private hands. The decision taken by Derby City Council on 14th December 1988 to put its Transport Company on the open market came, therefore, as something of a surprise both to the industry and the travelling public of Derby. Had the Conservatives not gained an overall majority of two seats in the previous May's elections, the decision may never have been taken.

The Council resolution did, however, agree to 'give favourable consideration to a management buy-out and any bids that promoted employee participation'. Employee participation, or for that matter ownership, had been given little headway throughout the NBC sales. Some of the more generous and dynamic management buy-outs had welcomed employee shareholders, albeit in a controlled minority. Others had paid scant regard to the role of their major assets. This, to their eventual cost, was the attitude of the DCT management team led by Peter Crook. Recognising the political bonus points to be gained by even cosmetic employee ownership, the management had held a series of meetings in January 1989 in an attempt to gain the workforce's backing. They explained that the five-man management team intended to raise around £250,000 and for that would expect to hold 51% of the equity. Their financial backers, at that stage unnamed, would pledge at least £1.75m and required at least 40% of the shares. They felt the asking price for the Company would be around £2.5m and, therefore, the remaining £500,000 would be subscribed by the employees, in return for which, they could have a stake of 9% of the shares.

The employees reaction was not surprising: Management £0.25m = 51%, Employees £0.5m = 9% did not sound like a good deal. The employee involvement was being sought reluctantly and this view was enforced by a comment attributed to one of the DCT managers who allegedly said to the employee gathering, "We would rather not have your money at all and we shall be seeing if we can raise the shortfall elsewhere".

This was enough for the majority of the employees and had prompted the Works Convenor and the Chairman of the local T&GWU branch to find an alternative course of action. They held a straw poll that indicated a large section of the workforce would support an employee bid. They had also read in the press that similar moves were being made in Clydeside and they had discovered that a former NBC Company had been involved in that bid. By the end of 17th February, the Derby drivers had met Graham Cumming and the following day an initial letter of interest was submitted to the Council's agents.

The bid team had readily recognised the need for professional leadership if their bid was to have any chance of success and my municipal background gave them some comfort. I was given a list of everything that was wrong, in their eyes, with DCT, and in particular why they could not support the management in their bid. Our first meeting was an unusual interview but I knew I was being weighed up so it was pleasing to hear from Graham the next day that I had passed the test.

My knowledge of Derby was scant considering I only lived 25 miles away and, as soon as I had finished at LCB, I set about understanding the network by spending days travelling around the bus routes. The original Derby network was fairly compact, nothing went more than four miles from the City Centre Morledge Bus Station, but it had always been a fairly healthy business and it would be a challenge to invent improvements. To keep in daily contact with Luton I was given a mobile telephone the size of a brick. It was a little embarrassing when it would ring on the top deck of a bus.

At a mass meeting on 12th March, I was paraded before the future shareholders amidst considerable propaganda from the existing management. My message was simple: long term commitment was essential, no promises, no guarantees, just hard work to succeed. I should choose the remaining members of the management team who should always be free to manage and I needed an overwhelming commitment by the workforce to subscribe to and support the buy-out. By the end of the meeting, over two-thirds of the workforce had pledged their money to the employee bid.

The following months were a continuous round of meetings with financial advisers, bank managers and regular late night meetings with the buy-out committee of twelve drivers and two engineers. The media enjoyed the prospect of a showdown between the existing management and their employees and many stories, mostly fabricated, dominated the airwaves and newspaper columns. There was a growing feeling of desperation from the DCT management and regular, if not half-hearted, attempts were made to win the workforce back. When that failed, less than subtle questions on my ability and recent background were resorted to.

We were also conscious that, in the event of our success, we would need to put together a new management team, as the incumbents were already tarred by their animosity to the employees bid. It was hard work without any guarantee that it would have a happy ending but working with the two senior reps, Iain and John, was refreshing. Their ambition was genuine and they were honest about their own shortcomings. They knew that without experienced leadership, no bank or financier would give their bid a second look and whilst they were encouraged by the amount of commitment, moral and monetary, that they were getting from their own members, this was small beer to what needed to be funded externally.

The first closure date for bids was 12th April and the BBC announced that the Council had received fourteen. By the end of the month we learnt that we had been shortlisted and would be allowed into the information data room at the beginning of May. Whilst there was great pre-occupation with who else had been shortlisted and how many, the real work to put together our definitive bid was becoming onerous.

The Council announced their intention to extend the shortlist from its original three to seven. This was not a decision we wanted to hear. Alongside the employees were the management bid and the weight of the former NBC empire: Trent, Midland Fox, Northern General, Potteries Motor Traction and Stevensons of Uttoxeter now under the control of Julian Peddle. We were particularly surprised by the inclusion of Trent who, if successful, would achieve a monopoly in Derby, and separate bids from Stevensons and Midland Fox who, by then, were 30% owned by Stevensons.

We had long since concluded that the winning bid had to be far greater than the DCT management's estimate of £2.5m and would more likely be in the region of

Graham Cumming, Managing Director of Luton & District Transport and Chairman of Derby City Transport Limited.

Like Leicester, Derby took delivery of Dennis Dominators, both with Marshall, as seen here on No. 104 (GTO 104V), and Northern Counties bodywork, but soon moved on to other manufacturers. *(DC)*

From 1984 Volvo's B10M model was the preferred choice, this example, No. 129 (A129 DTO) having bodywork by East Lancs. *(DC)*

Seen leaving Derby on the service acquired from Tailby & George (Blue Bus Services) in 1973, Marshall-bodied Volvo B10M carries a promotional livery for the operator's non-stage carriage activities. *(DC)*

£4 million. That meant significant borrowing at a time when the bank base rate was 14% and we were being quoted 3% to 5% above base rate for any borrowing.

Employee contributions had ranged from £160 to £30,000 but our reliance was firmly on the National Westminster Bank. Final bids were due to be lodged on the last day of June. Five days later we were called to the Council offices to be told that the employees offer was the preferred bid; that the present management would stand down and the Council would appoint me as Acting Managing Director until the legal work was completed. I was working for a council-owned company again.

That evening a meeting of the buy-out committee was arranged to be told the news. The initial gasp of incredulity and then the sense of over-powering euphoria had to be experienced to be believed. There had been so much negative press and scaremongering in the lead up to the final bids, I think that some of my colleagues had already resigned themselves to defeat, although no one would openly admit it. The news that, against considerable odds, they had succeeded where their management, their long-time competitor Trent and others had failed was overwhelming and some of the team were close to tears. In the end, £100,000 had been the difference between success and failure. Our bid of almost £3.75m had been accepted with no preference shown and no discounts. The employees had won by submitting the highest and the best bid.

Completion was finally reached on 25th August. The employees (55% of them including the new management team) had raised £454,000 and were rewarded with 75% of the shareholding. Luton and District would hold 25% by subscribing £151,000 and an unsecured loan of £650,000. The remainder of the asking price was to be realised by loans from the National Westminster Bank and the sale and leaseback of some of the fleet.

Individually, the Directors were expected by the Bank to shoulder the hardest financial burden. Whilst our colleagues at National Westminster wanted to be supportive, they also wanted to be certain that the leaders of the new Company were fully committed. Mortgaging your home was seen as a level of exposure that showed that commitment. Having so recently been faced with the possibility of losing our home, making a decision to use it as collateral in a venture that was highly dependent on the motivation of a group of bus drivers, may have seemed reckless in the extreme. But Barbara knew that this was my 'comeback' opportunity and whilst I had little right to expect it, given what we had so recently gone through, her support was, as usual, total.

Graham Cumming took on the Chairman's role of the new DCT and we recruited a new Engineer, Ken Bickle, a former Crosville colleague. We had to look outside for a Finance Director and fell lucky when we found Andrew Jarratt. The immediate problems facing the new Company in August 1989 were high interest rates and competition. The Bank base rate at that time was 14%; a month after completion it had risen to 15% – loans were all above base rate, one of the unsecured loans attracted 19% interest.

The euphoria needed to be converted into hard work and rapid change. One of our neighbours, a Drawlane subsidiary, Midland Red North (MRN) based at Cannock, had decided on an alternative strategy to the risk of a failing bid. They had registered competing services in Derby and planned to raid our new business with minibuses – shades of Fox Cubs all over again. And who was behind this assault? Hilditch had joined Drawlane and his son Christopher was in charge at Cannock.

The Derby employees were not about to let victory be grasped from them and readily accepted major operational changes and the introduction of minibus work – previously resisted in the former municipality. Our competitors knew that we were vulnerable and perceived our financial weakness to be our ultimate downfall. What they did not anticipate was the determination of the new shareholders. It was their company now and no one was going to take it away from them.

There were some doubting Thomases in the canteen but they were quickly dealt with by their colleagues. During the first eighteen months we increased service levels by 14% but reduced staff by seventy-five. The double-deck fleet had been reduced by twenty but replaced by thirty-three mini and midibuses. In its first full year the new DCT increased its turnover by 5% and managed to pay off almost £1m of its bank loans. But competition remained the biggest threat.

DCT operated a number of school buses that returned to depot between the peaks. We decided to take the fight to Midland Red and a small fleet of double-decks was despatched daily to Tamworth, MRN's nearest stronghold, to retaliate. Their reputation in Tamworth was not good and locals were pleased to see the new blue buses giving MRN a bloody nose. MRN's appetite for competition proved to be short-lived and they eventually sought peace and a deal which brought them out of Derby.

They had, however, drawn attention to our market and it was not long before a second wave of competition arrived, this time in the shape of a small family owned, Nottingham based company called Camms. They persisted for nearly two years, at one point sending seventeen buses daily from Nottingham to Derby to cream off our most lucrative routes. We knew they were not financially strong yet they were allowed to undermine our efforts to build the network. Eventually their Bank Manager took control and a deal was brokered to buy their business.

We had inherited the DCT telephone number, Derby 757575, amongst all the other assets and one day I off-handedly suggested it sounded like a good number for a taxi firm. Competition from taxis in Derby was rife and there was an immediate reaction amongst my colleagues that we could take the competition to the taxi companies. There are times when I should keep my thoughts to myself but the idea blossomed with the usual outburst of enthusiasm and it was not long before '75 Taxis' was born and the other taxi companies were retaliating by picking up at bus stops and (illegally) charging individual fares! Despite this, the ranks of '75 Taxis' grew from six to sixty although I never understood the economics of taxi operation and I was never convinced that it contributed in any significant way to the strength of DCT.

Iain Wordsworth and John Tidbury had been the founding fathers of the idea that employee ownership could work and could make money. They had a vision that a professionally run organisation, with the strength of employee backing, would be successful. They were right. The challenges, not the least of which was the price of money, were never-ending but their enthusiasm never waned. For Iain, who had devoted so much of his personal life to achieving the buy-out, it was as if he had achieved his goal and needed to scale new heights. He did this by up-rooting his young family and moving to Northern Scotland. John later followed him to open his own business in a remote Scottish village but stayed with DCT through its evolution and, I think, grew his own management skills as well.

We were constantly on the lookout for new opportunities and particularly ways of utilising the cavernous aircraft hangars that were our premises on Ascot Drive. Like Leicester we had continued to maintain the Council's ancillary fleet and had the joys of procuring everything from lawn mowers to dust carts. But just like Leicester the business was never going to support the overheads and we had to look elsewhere to fill the yawning space. The result was three Budget Rent-a-car franchises, in Derby, Lincoln and Grantham and the conversion of the ground floor of the former head office building to house Ascot Auto Sales. The car rental business requires a rapid turnover of vehicles and therefore a surplus of relatively new though, in some cases, high mileage cars that we could sell on to the second hand market. We had no embarrassment at becoming second hand car salesmen anymore than taking a slice of our competitors market, whether it was taxis or the private car.

Our venture into Lincolnshire had arisen when, in late 1991, we received a call from the union official at Lincoln City Transport, whose council were considering selling its bus company and whose employees thought that Luton and Derby was the model to follow. The problem was that this LCT was financially very precarious. There had been a long rivalry with the former NBC subsidiary Lincolnshire Road Car, which had been one of the last companies to be privatised. Frank Carter, the Chairman and Managing Director of Yorkshire Traction, had picked it up for a song and knew that, if he waited long enough, LCT would also fall into his hands. Given the animosity and the competition issues he knew he would not be allowed to bid openly for it, but also believed LCT was unsaleable on the open market.

The shareholders at Derby were anxious to help their beleaguered colleagues in Lincoln so we tried to put together a plan that would meet everyone's ambitions and still make money. Members of the DCT buy-out committee were keen to help persuade the employees in Lincoln to part with their savings, although it was apparent from the start that their appetite was unlike Derby's. However, we were able to persuade the National Westminster Bank to come to Lincoln's aid and put together a cohesive offer that the Council accepted.

For the first few months I found myself living in Lincoln trying to find ways of improving the efficiency and the viability of the business. Road Car was perched in the neighbouring depot like a vulture waiting to swoop. Within months it became clear that the buy-out was not sustainable; the market in Lincoln was too small and in truth could only ever support one operator.

I decided to speak to Carter to see if there was a deal to be done. I knew this would not go down well with the LCT employees, particularly those who had bought shares, but a sale, sooner than later might, at least, protect their investment. In my conversation with Carter I also made it clear that, if DCT was going to deliver Road Car's rival into his hands, there had to be something in it for DCT. We agreed terms, DCT would receive an arrangement fee and LCT's employee investors would get their investment back but without profit.

This was a difficult message to deliver to the LCT employees who, for years, had maintained a dignified superiority over their rivals in Lincoln but were now faced with capitulation. For some it was too much and the position was about to worsen when, during the period of due diligence, Carter announced he would only pay 50p in the pound. This was twisting the knife, but we had gone too far and in reality there was only ever going to be one outcome to LCT's problems. So after only 16 months of employee-ownership, LCT was sold to Carter who, at the death, also reneged on his agreement to pay DCT for their involvement in delivering the monopoly of Lincoln to him.

Ironically, it was about this time that my former employers finally decided that privatisation could no longer be avoided and a decision had been taken to put Leicester CityBus on the open market. My buy-out colleagues were keen to make a play for LCB and initial talks with their counterparts at Abbey Park Road were encouraging.

I was the tasked to write to the City Council, expressing our interest in developing our successful model of employee-ownership with their employees in the hope that it might give a joint DCT/LCB employee bid an inside track. The response was polite but not unexpected. The Company was to be offered to any interested party and we must take our chances in the competition. I was very tempted at that point to suggest to my colleagues that we adopt the Midland Red North 'model' and begin competing in Leicester but they were keen to put together a legitimate bid with the Leicester buy-out team, which is what we did. Whilst we achieved the shortlist, it was not long before we suspected we had stronger competition than in Derby. Our advisors were adamant that we could not go much higher than £4m; in the event LCB was sold for an inflated £7m to the emerging Grampian Transport from Aberdeen who, through two further iterations, became First Group.

There were two more DCT efforts to expand which might, if they had succeeded, have changed the shape of later developments in the industry. Dunn-Line was a family owned business in Nottingham led by the father, Bob Dunn. He was clearly entrepreneurial and had recognised the opportunities that lay in the heart of a dormant municipality in sprawling Nottingham. We approached Bob and started talks about a possible acquisition although the prospect of financing a deal would be more of a challenge than agreeing it. Bob was a canny fellow and the negotiations were often long and detailed. His main objective was always to secure the future for his wife and sons. Our advisors came into their own when they devised a proposal that, in effect, financed the deal from Dunn-Line's own revenues. We were at the final meeting with lawyers before signing when Bob finally got cold feet and pulled out.

The second deal that could have changed the course of history was our attempt to buy Trent. During the five years of employee ownership, my relationship with Brian King had been cordial and for all his old-fashioned ways, I had an enduring respect for him as an individual. Trent was shrewdly led by Brian, with a strong number two in Ian Morgan. Their business was consistently profitable and the surprising acquisition of Barton Transport had strengthened their hold on the Nottinghamshire, Derbyshire market. We felt the merger of our organisations could take their development to the next level.

The discussions we held in a hotel in Castle Donington, next to East Midlands Airport, were entertaining but not overly productive. I grew increasingly to believe that Brian, although we had offered him the Chairmanship of the new conglomeration, would always be his own boss and would be unlikely to give Trent up easily. The talks came to naught and Brian continued to lord over his little empire, regularly to be courted by the ever-expanding Groups, but never really wanting to relinquish his seat.

I think there must come a point in employee ownership when the novelty wears thin and reality sets in. For the first three years or so, following the historic decision of Derby City Council to sell its bus company to its employees, the relationships at all levels in DCT had cemented and worked to the common good. The drivers faced and accepted many changes, often those that, as municipal employees, they had resisted vociferously. But that cannot be milked forever. It had been hard work surviving competition from the outset, facing incredibly high finance charges and searching for any small opening to grow the business. Without growth the Company would find it difficult to survive independently long term and, to grow effectively, it needed the confidence to raise more investment.

Already some of the early NBC management buy-outs had reached this point and the big Groups were beginning to emerge through a second round of buy-outs; in some cases, shortly before the originals failed completely. The art is knowing when to cash in your chips and, as we approached our sixth year of independence, we had options to consider that we knew might not be available forever. So I was deployed to approach some of the big-hitters and see if DCT interested them as an addition to their ever-growing portfolios.

Breakfast with Stagecoach's Brian Souter over eggs Benedict in an expensive London hotel was an experience and, yes, he did arrive in trainers, carrying a Tesco shopping bag. Discussions with David Martin, by then, in the ascendancy at British Bus (formerly Drawlane), were also always interesting as David developed his reputation for, quite literally, doing deals on the back of his fag packet.

The DCT buy-out committee were at first sceptical about where our future lay and Graham Cumming and I, sometimes, had our work cut out to keep them on board. Like their colleagues in Lincoln, their greatest fear was the possibility of being sold to their arch-rivals, Trent. Grampian, having acquired Leicester, was another option but they were already stretched by that deal, so the serious talking fell to Drawlane.

Negotiations finally led to a meeting with Chairman Dawson Williams, Gordon Watts and David Martin in Cannock where agreement was reached, in principle, to deal solely with British Bus and David and I were left to fight over the details. We reached an offer of £3.30 for each £1 share which, for a five year investment, seemed a reasonable return so I was faced with persuading those who had courageously followed me into the unknown world of share ownership in 1989, to now relinquish those shares and become employees of a larger group.

It was a poignant occasion, and not surprisingly, there was some opposition particularly from those who still smarted from the then Drawlane-owned Midland Red North's spoiling tactics in the very early days of employee ownership. But the majority recognised that their investment, against sizeable odds, had made a return and many thanked me genuinely for making more money for them than they had ever anticipated when we had set out together. The deal was done and David, either mischievously or with great forethought, presented me with my new challenge.

A final gathering of shareholders took place at the Midland Hotel in Derby on 5th August to celebrate the deal and reminisce. We had gone through a lot together: competition, scepticism, opposition and sky-high bank rates but the camaraderie and determination had sustained for five years and those who had put their faith in he employee buy-out concept had been rightly rewarded.

By the time the decision to sell Derby City Transport was taken, the fleet purchasing policy had settled on the Volvo B10M chassis, with Northern Counties bodies, as seeen here, No. 147 (C147 NRR). *(DC)*

Lincoln purchased three of these East Lancs-bodied Leyland Olympians in 1985 and had them fitted with coach seating. They passed to Frank Carter's Yorkshire Traction group on the sale of the business. *(DC)*

The original North Western Road Car Company was formed in 1923 and was based in Macclesfield. For many years Bristol L5G models were a familiar part of the single-deck fleet, as typified by No. 270 (BJA 425) with Willowbrook 38-seat body. *(JR)*

The final type of double-decker delivered to the original North Western company were Daimler Fleetlines with Alexander 75-seat bodies. *(JS)*

Chapter 6 – The North Western Years

British Bus had already gained its reputation before I became one of its employees. Competitors were convinced that their strategy was to quickly amass volume, with the minimum of investment and, if there were assets to strip on the way, that was a bonus. Their early acquisitions had been the leftovers of the great NBC sale – those that even the incumbent directors could not finance. Some were secondary sales that the initial purchasers could not sustain and fell willingly into the then Drawlane's hands. Ironically with an engineer, Dawson Williams, at its helm, the lack of investment reflected sadly on its fleet and their maintenance standards.

Once the Derby deal had been completed, it was apparent that British Bus would want its own people in and after a short handing over period, it was time for me to move on. I can't remember how strongly David suggested Liverpool as my next post, but my reaction was that I would go but, given the uncertainty of British Bus's future, I would not uproot my family from Leicestershire. I was uncertain of the longevity of any position in British Bus, and my job security had yet to be tested.

It didn't deter him so, on 3rd October 1994, I embarked on my first trek up the M6. It was a good three hour journey, as the A50 link between the M1 and M6 was yet to be built and the first half of the journey, from Leicester to Stoke, was cross-country, often through a maze of country lanes to avoid a crawl through another overly congested market town.

My predecessor, Bob Gregory, was already out of favour and was being condemned to dealing with uniform supply and anything else that no one wanted to pick up. Without a portfolio, your days are always numbered. North Western was a mixed bag of operational oddities. It had the remnants of the southerly part of the original Ribble Motor Services, depots at Wigan, Skelmersdale, Aintree and Bootle; the former Crosville depots that had been discarded by the original North Western Road Car, Runcorn, Warrington and Winsford and a Manchester operation that had an 'under the arches' base just off the Chester Road with two outlying depots in Rochdale and Oldham.

Despite extreme measures of austerity, (even Long Service Awards had been cancelled to save money) much of its operation was fragmented and losing money. The fleet was the subject of intense interest from the regulating authorities and the management had just managed to keep one step ahead of a Public Inquiry. That was until I arrived.

Competition was chaotic in and around Liverpool from a number of totally undisciplined private operators and a slowly disintegrating PTE-owned monopoly, Merseybus. Bizarrely, even within North Western, neighbouring depots competed for lucrative corridors so that both Bootle and Aintree depots could be seen fighting each other on the grossly over-bussed routes between Liverpool and St Helens. Its Liverline acquisition, located yards from the North Western depot in Hawthorne Road in Bootle, was happy to compete with everyone, even if they were family.

What North Western did have were some quality people who knew the industry well but who needed direction. It was clear that an outsider had to prove himself, and my allegiance to one of the football clubs immediately gained me some credibility, at least with half of the staff. The same could not be said for the trade union reaction to their new Managing Director. Liverpool may have had a long-time image of 'bolshie' trade unions and militancy, and I have to confess my earlier experience during my first visit as a trainee did nothing to dispel this reputation, but there were some local representatives that made an art of preserving that image.

I decided, rather recklessly, to hold a series of employee meetings (roadshows) to introduce myself and present my thoughts and ambitions for the future of North Western. The first of these roadshows was to be at Bootle, probably the company's most notorious depot, and arrangements were made to hold the meeting at a working men's club close to the depot in Hawthorne Road. Whilst I had hoped for a reasonable turnout, my expectations were not high so I was more than a little shocked when I arrived at the Mel Inn to find upward of 200 employees crammed into a room that did not have a single window, or an obvious easy escape route.

The gathering listened in silence to my presentation and when I invited questions I received the first of many tirades from their union representative 'Chalky' White who lambasted me, and everything I represented, for a full twenty minutes without drawing breath. Needless to say, until that evening, I had never set eyes on Chalky or he on me but that did not deter him from questioning everything I stood for and he, as a Liverpool trade union rep, was duty-bound to revile. I had been met in silence, he was received with ovation.

We had arranged refreshments for the attendees in the form of a Lancashire hotpot that emerged from the gents' toilets where staff were washing the plates and cutlery and by the end of the evening, although physically unscathed, I really wondered what David Martin had condemned me to.

Although Chalky always maintained his union persona in public forums, he was the most pleasant of characters to talk to on a one-to-one basis and I was even more surprised to learn much later that he was an accomplished artist. He confided in me that this was his outlet for the pressures of being a TU rep and I confess that, if his rantings at me resulted in the brilliant paintings he produced, I was happy to contribute to such a talent.

British Bus was still surviving on a shoestring and financial reviews at its head office in Salisbury were never relished. My first as North Western's new MD set the scene and the culture according to the Directors, Dawson Williams, Gordon Watt and, of course, David Martin. Over dinner the evening prior to our meeting, Dawson Williams suggested that those municipalities still in public ownership were weak enough to exploit and concluded that a short period of intense competition would batter the likes of Warrington or Halton into early submission, when a deal to buy them would be their only way out. As the only party to this conversation who had experience of municipal thinking, I was more than a little concerned that the British Bus management was in danger of under-estimating the resilience of council pride.

It was clear, however, that I was in a minority of one and, as the new boy, I was never going to exercise a great deal of influence when minds were already made up. To be fair, my new colleagues at North Western could also see the flaws in such a strategy, but they knew more than me when not to argue with Dawson. I expressed my concerns, they were politely noted, but the following morning it was decided that we would start plans to compete with Warrington Borough Transport.

The Regional Director, to whom I reported, was Richard (Dickie) Bowler, ex-NBC, formerly from South Midlands. A nice enough man but heavily inclined to not rocking the boat. I knew from an early stage that I was unlikely to get any support in an argument with the board, so 'go with the flow' seemed the safest option. My concerns proved to be prophetic.

The plan was to set up a dedicated unit in Warrington to start the offensive and Alf Lloyd, who had been running Liverline so had a competitive spirit, was selected to recruit and head the unit. We would offer some degree of quality with new buses; the Warrington Corporation fleet was tired and under-invested, and we would be competitive on fares and frequency. So 'Warrington Goldline' was born.

George Hurst was in charge at Warrington, an engineer who could be belligerent, and was understandably unhappy when I was deployed to discuss the scenario of a British Bus takeover, either peacefully or by force. Under normal circumstances I was certain that George was not the best motivator in the world, but threats of extinction from one of the big boys, soon focused his and his employees' minds. He retaliated by competing on routes into Liverpool and St Helens and it soon became apparent that this 'short period of intense competition' was likely to develop into something rivalling the hundred years war.

George probably secured more political support than he had experienced in his whole career; the rest of the municipal family encouraged Warrington to survive at all costs. The battle dragged on; in the first year alone it cost British Bus over a million pounds and whilst we could see that the opposition was struggling, the political will was growing and rather than reach an agreement with their aggressors they became more determined to fight to the death. In fact at times, I got the impression that they would set fire to everything rather than do a deal with British Bus.

The propaganda war was also often dirty. A staff notice appeared on the WBT noticeboards displaying an extract from 'The Guardian' newspaper relating to an alleged £1m loan the British Bus Chairman Dawson Williams had received from the Bank of Boston and which was now being investigated by the Office of Serious Fraud. The article also suggested that British Bus owed the Bank of Boston £110m which must have convinced the WBT employees reading it that British Bus and its competition in Warrington were not long for this world. In the end we were forced to back down and orchestrate a gradual re-entrenchment. It was some time, and a change of management, before Warrington Corporation was able to recover and the people of Warrington gained little from the experience other than a confirmed hatred of big bullies.

There were more sensible opportunities to expand, as a number of smaller operators, who had emerged post deregulation, were ready to cash in their chips. So for two or three years, Phil Stone, who at that time was my Finance Director at Aintree, and I did the rounds and soon accumulated the likes of Little White Bus in Ormskirk, Wigan Bus, Loftys in Chester and not for the last time Martin Bott and Dave Stewart's South Lancashire Transport. One of the more interesting acquisitions was Starline Travel in Knutsford. Simon Fawcett, the then owner, did not want anyone to know we were talking to him or that he was considering selling. So he insisted that the only time that Phil and I could look at the books was late

North Western's head office was based at Aintree, where the depot had formerly belonged to Ribble Motor Services, prior to another example of the NBC's 'divide and sell' policy.

The TRN registration on North Western's No. 616 provides an undisputable clue as to its origins with Ribble. Together with 340 buses and four former Ribble garages, the new North Western was sold to Drawlane in March 1988. It is seen close to Greater Manchester Museum of Transport during that month. *(IS)*

at night. We complied and visited his premises at midnight and, in due course, the acquisition became the basis of Arriva North West's interests in South Manchester.

The fleet at North Western was in poor shape. There had been no investment since British Bus ownership and engineering standards were not good. The company had managed deftly to stay one step ahead of VOSA, the vehicle standards inspectorate and, whenever challenged (or threatened) by the regulatory body's scrutiny, it had pumped resources in and, some would say, fire-fought its way out of a Public Inquiry. It was inevitable that this situation could not be sustained and just when we thought we were actually coming to grips with our engineering deficiencies, VOSA descended on the depot at Skelmersdale and I was in court. I am not proud to admit that over the years I have appeared before more than my fair share of Public Inquiries and may have achieved an unwanted reputation with some Traffic Commissioners, but a Public Inquiry for engineering shortcomings is probably the worst type of experience any Operator's Licence holder can have.

A Public Inquiry is what it says; your dirty washing is exhibited in public and your personal failures, because you are the designated Transport Manager, are laid out for all to see. What is worse, when the Inquiry is engineering related, is the undertone that your business is unsafe. I have never worked for a bus company that did not put safety as its primary objective, both for its customers and in the workplace, but poor engineering standards inevitably suggest unsafe vehicles. It was a day I was eager never to repeat; we received a fair penalty of a 10% reduction in our licences. Although I have worked with many competent and professional engineers, I have always demanded the highest standards of maintenance for a purely selfish reason – never to experience again an engineering Public Inquiry.

On the positive side, British Bus finally recognised the overdue need to invest in new buses and in September 1995 we received a batch of fifty Dennis Darts. Pleased with the impact that these could make on the public transport landscape in Liverpool, we invited the Chairman of the Passenger Transport Authority, Mark Dowd, to officially launch the new 'CityPlus' vehicles. Whilst gracious in his welcome of a sizeable investment, he confided to me afterwards that he wished they could have been the new low-floor type of bus! The PTE had invested in 14 low-floor Scanias at twice the price of the Darts. Despite their unknown pedigree, the 'step' Darts survived much longer than anyone expected. The Scanias were problematic from their arrival.

The Passenger Transport Authority and Executive, Merseytravel, was a powerful but frustrated body. Roy Swainson was its kindly and approachable Director General who almost perfected the eternal political juggling act between the controlling Labour Party, headed by the PTA's Chairman Mark Dowd, and the demands of the five Metropolitan districts that comprised the PTA. At the centre of these was Liverpool that, having suffered some of the worst forms of left wing politics for more than a decade, was now decidedly Liberal. Although the Wirral, Southport and St Helens councils had their own particular problems and demands, Liverpool was inevitably the focal point that determined PTA policy and the success or failure of that policy. Privatisation had not been well received on Merseyside and whilst the employee-ownership of Merseybus was tolerable, the likes of British Bus and the emerging groups were much less so. Swainson tried to maintain harmony between this impossible mix of operators and politicians and to strike some balance between reality and the, sometimes outrageous, ambitions of the ruling group. He was the master of compromise but his political masters wanted someone more dynamic.

Merseytravel's closest rival, Manchester, had emerged from the post-war era to justify its position as the country's third city and even the IRA bomb in 1997 did not deter its ambitions. The re-development of the City Centre had much to thank the terrorists for. In transport terms, the Metrolink tram system gave it 'European status' and despite the questionable economics of the modern day tram, Manchester and its PTA forged their whole public transport strategy around the re-introduction of the tram. Consequently, thirty miles away, Liverpool lived in the shadow of Manchester and resented it. Liverpool had is own light rail dreams; the Light Rail Group, headed by Professor Lewis Lesley of Liverpool John Moores University, had ambitious ideas that were totally unaffordable. But the politicians wanted something to steal the limelight from their neighbours up the East Lancashire Road.

Neil Scales had arrived as Operations Director at the PTE's headquarters in Hatton Garden, and it was soon clear that he was destined for higher places. A 'simple Geordie engineer' was his self-description, but he had an ability to deliver and above all he was visionary. It was not long before he displaced Swainson and set about regenerating Merseytravel. His ability to manage his politicians was educational but his ability to deliver funding and consequently a project was, at times, breathtaking. He was not well liked at the Department for Transport, but his persuasion rarely ended in failure when he needed to finance his latest scheme. His ambition to rival and overtake Manchester was singular and a tram system was to be the central plank of his plan.

The bus companies saw this as a threat and in North Western there was a high degree of scepticism. Nevertheless we tried to be constructive in developing, what we considered to be, a more practical approach to the vision and advocated the more flexible version of a trolleybus system. Despite considerable hard work and patience, Neil was not persuaded and he was determined to pursue his tram dream. His plans battled through much iteration, numerous planning applications and inevitably truncated versions but, having spent tens of millions, he failed to persuade the DfT to release the finance needed for the project. It was a bitter defeat and for a while coloured the PTA's attitude more darkly where the bus operators were concerned. In retrospect it may have been a welcome catalyst in the evolution of PTE/Operator relationships. Although it took some time to get the people at Merseytravel to focus on the day job and the basic need to use the bus more effectively, that relationship started, very gradually, to improve and, although the PTE later had the opportunity for greater control over the private sector (Quality Contracts), it did not rush into that confrontation.

Meanwhile, British Bus had run its course. It had stayed one step ahead of its creditors and, with a fairly substantial portfolio, or a mixed bag of operations some might say, a deal was done for Cowies, the motor dealership, to acquire the business. Cowies, whose total bus involvement at that time ran to their extensive presence in London, saw this as a platform for developing in the public transport market; British Bus saw money. It was a surprising alliance and amongst our contemporaries in the industry, there was much bewilderment and not a little scepticism. A company, whose North East roots were in motorcycles, seemed to be punching way above its weight. The idea that it could invade the tradition of running buses by acquiring the least attractive (low cost) option that British Bus had become, cemented the belief that Cowies had a lot to learn and its education may prove expensive.

The new business was able to shed some of its notoriety: Dawson Williams bowed out and into jail and Gordon Watts moved into other fields. David Martin survived the reputation that had tarnished British Bus and moved in to start expanding Cowies on a wider field. Steve Clayton, Cowies man in London, was given the opportunity to venture out of the capital and rein in the ex-British Bus contingent and David was allowed to explore the opportunities across the Channel, provided, it was suggested, that opportunity was no further than an hour's flight on a low cost airline.

Gordon Hodgson was the Chief Executive of Cowies. It was evident from the start that his knowledge or interest of buses was limited. He insisted, however, that he would chair the quarterly finance reviews of each of his newly gained subsidiaries and we were summoned to a hotel on the Welsh border to perform.

Hodgson was best described as a slightly younger model of the young Mr Grace in the television series 'Are You Being Served'. He only ever left the Cowies head office in Sunderland with his Personal Assistant Linda and gave the impression that 'you're all doing very well' would be sufficient to make his audience believe that he understood everything we had told him.

On this occasion we had been analysing figures for about an hour when there was a knock on the hotel room door and a nurse appeared wheeling in a hospital drip. The momentary silence, as everyone digested this scene, seemed to last for ever. Eventually, the nurse realised her mistake and left. We, however, remained convinced the equipment had been sent to support Gordon and had to restrain ourselves for another two hours before we were able, well away from the hotel, to fall about with helpless laughter. Future finance reviews suffered greatly from that meeting and it was always difficult to treat the events seriously when, at any moment, we expected medical help to appear through the door.

In early 1998, the senior management of the group were summoned to Birmingham to have revealed the newly designed livery that was to accompany the re-naming of the Cowie Group to 'Arriva'. Whilst it took some time for the world to accept that Arriva was not pronounced Arrive-a, the bigger shock was the announcement that our buses were to be painted turquoise. Now the bus industry has long been traditional in its liveries so that reds and greens had dominated for decades. There had been some adventurous diversions involving whites and blues but generally we have been a conservative bunch and rarely strayed from primary colours.

Ray Stenning, of Best Impressions, delights in being outrageous. He is rewarded by gasps and exclamations. His appearance in motorcycle leathers (probably a generous gesture to Cowies about-to-be-obliterated image) discarded to reveal a string vest and tight shorts, was the prelude to a fascinating afternoon. The new livery was described as aquamarine and stone. It looked like turquoise; you don't paint buses in pastel colours. Everyone hated it; no one said anything. We left wondering if we would be supplied with corporate sunglasses to disguise our relationship with the new livery. And yet it was hailing a new era. The old Cowie regime was gradually and subtly being dismantled and in its place, the chrysalis of a European company was emerging with acquisitions in Spain and Portugal pointing towards Italy and Germany and the new eastern horizon emerging from the Soviet break up.

At home, Hodgson retired and a new Chief Executive, devoid of any transport background, Bob Davies, took his place. Sunderland was still seen as the centre of the Group but the UK bus sector, under Steve Clayton, created its own head office in Leicester and fragmentation seemed to be quietly acceptable. The Group remained in the shadow of First Group and Stagecoach, however. They had both developed quickly during the 'nineties through acquisition and success in rail franchising. Arriva did not run trains and the Stock Exchange and business analysts regarded it as second division. This was to change, but not necessarily in the way we had anticipated.

Introduction of CityPlus

Chapter 7 – The Arriva Years

Merseybus, Merseyside Transport Ltd Holdings, had ambitions beyond their reach. The employee-owned, formerly PTE-owned, company had dominated the bus market on Merseyside but yearned to be a bigger player. There had been some local bus consolidation and they had dabbled in London but they too saw rail as their answer to 'street cred'. Unfortunately, their success in winning the Merseyrail and Northern Spirit franchises brought more baggage and more problems than they had expected. The two franchises were the rump of the rail privatisation process and were not the prizes that the Intercity companies offered. Inevitably, bus companies moving into rail were going to be dependent on the rail personnel, many of whom had aspired to buy-outs, most of whom treated their cousins in the bus industry with disdain.

It was not long before MTL was being dragged down slowly by the enormity of their entry into the rail sector. They needed a more substantial and profitable acquisition or to dispose. The second option was a bitter pill to swallow and for some time the Directors railed against the thought. Dominic Brady, MTL's Commercial Director, had been part of the Derek Hatton era of political turmoil in Liverpool and like all good left-wingers had grabbed a taste of capitalism when Merseybus was privatised. He had been deployed to run the group's London operations, but returned when that part of the business contracted. Despite his politics, he was a likeable Scouser and he and I enjoyed a strange relationship. He enjoyed referring to me, slightly derogatively, as the 'Busman' and I retaliated by deriding his football allegiances to the blue half of the city. Our respective relationships with the PTE and Neil Scales in particular, often made us unlikely allies and, in quieter moments over a beer, he admitted that MTL was running out of options and a sale was inevitable.

Meanwhile, two events placed us under the national spotlight for all the wrong reasons. A panel of operators chaired by the PTE, managed Merseyside's multi-operator, multi-journey, travelcard scheme. The Solo (bus) and Trio (bus and rail) tickets were very successful, because of their pricing and flexibility, but arguments over the pricing levels caused constant friction between the operators and the PTE, the latter wanting their range of tickets to be as cheap as possible, regardless of competing commercial fares.

The PTE also subsidised child fares and, at one meeting in an attempt to reduce their exposure, PTE officers asked the operators to come to some agreement over the level of fare that children should be charged commercially. At the PTE's request, an operator meeting subsequently took place to agree the fare. Despite the whole process being properly documented, the Office of Fair Trading became aware of our activity and accusations of cartels and price-fixing were levelled. Curiously, at this point, the PTE withdrew into the background and the operators were left to face the charges. We avoided jail but were sanctioned for the apparent collaboration and the relationship with the PTE deteriorated a further step.

The Traffic Commissioner has a strange role. Responsible to the Secretary of State, dependent on officials who they do not employ, their independence in policing the road transport industries is slightly unreal and one cannot help seeing them as judge and jury rolled into one body. Privatisation of the bus industry, greatly resented by Labour-controlled local authorities, had generated claims that the industry was putting profit before the customer and, in particular, service reliability and punctuality were the victims. There may have been some truth in these accusations, but many were deeply rooted in political dogma and often spurious. Competition, post deregulation, had seen improvements in service frequency, particularly in the conurbations and, after a reticent start, investment in quality. But the Councils saw their control dissipating and the big Groups becoming even more powerful. Inevitably, this strained all relationships, but mostly so with the Passenger Transport Executives.

Manchester enjoyed a variety of bus operators, all shapes and sizes. First Group had established itself in the north of the area with Stagecoach in the south and, intermingled, were a number of family businesses and unrealistic entrepreneurs and Arriva. Our operations in Manchester represented about 6% of the total market. We were a bit player and not the most reliable or attractive option for bus customers. The PTE saw the Traffic Commissioner as a certain way of bringing some of the mavericks to heel and actively encouraged service monitoring (timing checks). It came as no surprise that we were soon called to a Public Inquiry in Stretford in June 1999.

The hearing was presided over by the Deputy Traffic Commissioner Mark Hinchliffe. He could not have known that he was about to make history. Our advocate Geoffrey Jones, long established in the industry's legal wrangles, was the most loquacious and elegant of orators and did his best to lessen our guilt, but our shortcomings were obvious for all to see and we were judged to be guilty.

What was to make this decision monumental was the Deputy Traffic Commissioner's misguided attempt to be fair. Legislation clearly (and unreasonably) demands that every bus operator who registers a timetable is expected to comply with that registration to the letter and will be found in violation if the timetable is not fully delivered as registered. Hinchliffe, I'm sure trying to be helpful, determined that, perhaps, 100% compliance was unachievable and, to his mind, 95% of all services operating within a 'window' of one minute early to five minutes late, gave some scope and allowance for unforeseen delays and disruptions.

With that pronouncement, the industry became saddled with something worse than 100% compliance – a narrow set of parameters that his fellow Commissioners saw as a final concession to erring operators and, from then on, they were determined that the standard should be achieved, regardless of individual circumstances. The reality was that, in built up areas, punctuality levels could vary considerably. At that time, there was no accurate way of monitoring every single journey and every single timing point but best guesses put the average number of journeys falling within Hinchliffe's 'window of tolerance' between 75% and 80%. What had started as a magnanimous gesture on the part of the Deputy Traffic Commissioner was to become the greatest millstone around the industry's neck.

The PTEs smelt blood and whenever possible used this judgement to pressure operators in their area. The irony continues that 95% cannot be regularly achievable without strict traffic control measures (usually in the gift of the local authorities), that operating conditions vary day to day if not hour to hour, and the rail industry, not known for its congestion problems, considers inter-city trains, arriving within ten minutes of their advertised time, to be 'on time'.

The two rail franchises were beginning to eat into MTL's cash and despite the grandiose ambitions of its Chief Executive and Finance Director, talks started on a possible sale. The negotiations seemed never-ending and there was certainly resistance to the minnow swallowing the whale. But a deal loomed and by the start of 2000, it looked as if Arriva North West was about to be inflated five-fold. There was a resignation that we would not be able to retain MTL Holdings in its entirety, as the Monopolies Commission would certainly have a say in the outcome. So, to prevent a referral to the Commission, we decided to offer up our own sacrificial lamb representing about 10% of the business.

Gillmoss depot was identified as an option for divestment but David Martin was determined to keep as many of the profitable routes as possible. In January, I was on a skiing holiday in Austria while the deliberations crawled onward. I do not ski but my wife was determined that I should have lessons with her ski guide of many years. During my first attempt, my mobile rang: it was David wanting to discuss which Gillmoss routes were worth keeping. After two further interruptions, my instructor threw his hands up in frustration and abandoned me on the slope. My skiing progressed no further but the MTL deal did.

An Extraordinary General Meeting on 17th February decided its fate and overnight the Arriva business on Merseyside saw its turnover increase from £30m to £150m and we got two rail franchises as well! The deal had not come a moment too soon. Merseybus was leaking cash and could have gone into administration within weeks. This meant that our well-rehearsed action plan to consolidate the two businesses needed to be immediately effective. Within twenty-four hours of the acquisition, every one of MTL's former fleet had Arriva vinyls on them and an Arriva sign replaced Merseybus on every property we had acquired.

The cosmetics were easy; the economics were to prove slightly more difficult. Although the plan to take out more than 200 vehicles was delivered within six months, it was not without pain. When everyone expects change, give them change as quickly and as painlessly as possible. The meeting with all the local Merseybus management, the day after the takeover, was frosty to say the least. The resentment was palpable and the uncertainty, which for a long time had permeated MTL's structure, was now reality. We swung the axe swiftly and cleanly. We knew, from past relationships, which of the former management team would be assets and who would lead the resistance.

The meeting with MTL's union officials, ten days later, was almost surreal. The full time local official had arranged a meeting in Transport House in the City Centre. We entered a room where there were thirty representatives sitting, none of whom wanted to be there. We had inherited eight depots including Gillmoss, at Southport, Green Lane, St Helens, Huyton (Liverbus), Speke, Garston (Village Tours), and Birkenhead and we were about to find out what running buses on Merseyside was really about. Also in the 'job lot' was Heysham Travel in North Lancashire that was sold to Stagecoach Ribble soon after the acquisition. Talks continued on the divestment of Gillmoss that eventually happened in July when it was sold to a consortium led by Dominic Brady. Glenvale Transport was not going to make it easy for us to adapt to the mega company and any honeymoon, we thought we might enjoy, was short-lived when we introduced our new competitors.

The rail franchises had two more years to run. Northern Spirit had all sorts of problems exacerbated by staff shortages. Merseyrail was penalised for its punctuality; consequently its profit margin was greatly reduced. For a Group that wanted the kudos of running a railway, if not the baggage that comes with it, Arriva now found itself with two ailing businesses and little or no expertise within its own ranks to find a cure. There were obvious weaknesses with the Merseyrail management and its relationship with the PTE was not good. Neil Scales had long held the ambition that the Executive should be the franchising authority and Merseyrail should be returned to local accountability. His views were wholeheartedly supported by his Chairman Mark Dowd, himself a former railway worker.

On the whole Merseytravel had welcomed Arriva's acquisition of MTL, they saw Merseybus as greater opposition than Arriva, and the take-over had probably taken away the last vestiges of the political tensions between the PTA and its former undertaking. To be fair, Neil was very supportive as we were making sizeable changes to the structure of the network and suppressed, as far as he was able, any complaints from his local politicians.

The Group invited Euan Cameron, a veteran railwayman, to oversee the two rail franchises and he, together with Steve Clayton, suggested that political points were there to be won if we approached our newly expanded business on Merseyside as one entity. We had the opportunity to explore greater bus/rail co-ordination, an ambition high on the list of the PTE's priorities and delivering 'a single integrated network', one of Neil's favourite mantras. This could be the blueprint for future opportunities, without relinquishing too much control or involvement to the Executive. What we needed, therefore, was one person to bring together both the rail and bus businesses. This was not a job that appeared in the situations vacant; there was only one candidate and he did not have the opportunity to debate the proposition. With the bus side still coming to grips with the intricacies of consolidation, I was persuaded to add Merseyrail to my greatly expanded responsibilities.

If the reaction of the MTL bus management and union at being taken over by their smaller competitor was an experience, my first meeting with the management team of Merseyrail was unique. I know nothing about railways. In fact, I have little interest in railways. Throughout my career, the rail industry had always run on parallel lines to its cheaper cousin, the bus industry, and there had been little or no working relationship between the two. Certainly the rail industry has always treated the bus side with an aloof disdain and during my earlier years I was never aware of any managerial movement between the two industries.

But here I was, about to wear two hats, one of which I had never imagined in my worst nightmares, would ever fit me. The Merseyrail management was understandably bemused if not a little nervous about my appointment. They were welcoming, in an uncertain sort of way, but gradually realised there might be some benefit in educating someone who knew absolute zero about their company or the industry to which it belonged, and set about enlightening me.

The rail industry is built on acronyms. It has its own language, but my new colleagues were kind enough to translate as we went along and I soon grasped SRA (Strategic Rail Authority) and SPADs (Signal Passed at Danger) along with a hundred others. My first and lasting impression was how safety focused rail people are. In the bus industry we think we put safety first but the rail industry is fanatical. The safety regime presumes 100% compliance and therefore expects 100% safety levels. In the real world this just does not happen. People get in the way, human error plays its part but when the inevitable accident occurs in the rail industry, however minor or catastrophic, the same intensity is ignited through endless analysis, investigations and post-mortems.

Safety committees filled diaries, safety courses were an industry in themselves and the trades unions did their best to ensure that everything of any significance was safety-related. The local officials, Colin Smith for ASLEF and Andy Warnock-Smith for RMT, were approachable and willing to discuss issues sensibly but the central power base of the two unions was all-powerful. Most decisions had to be referred to London and this, inevitably, prolonged even the most trivial issues.

Merseyrail is essentially two lines: the Northern line crossing Liverpool from Southport in the north to Hunts Cross in the south, with two spurs to Ormskirk and Kirkby, and the Wirral line which runs from Liverpool city centre under the river Mersey then splits in three different directions to New Brighton, West Kirby and Chester. The services were well used, heavily subsidised, to about £3 per passenger journey, and almost entirely isolated from the rest of the nation's rail network. The fleet was ageing and with growing passenger numbers, the time spent at each station was causing increasing delays and time penalties.

I was assured that a tweak to the timetables' intermediate timing points would resolve this problem – it literally needed seconds being re-distributed across the timetable. When I naively asked why this had not been done already and how long it would take to implement, I was given a litany of reasons why it had been impossible. It would take 18 months to achieve, I was told, and when I replied that it had taken less than six months to revise the whole of the Merseyside bus network, I was met with the kind of facial expressions usually reserved for five year olds who are questioning the meaning of life. In the end we achieved the necessary changes in 9 months, a record in the minds of some of my new colleagues. It was, as the period suggests, as traumatic as giving birth.

Now that my time was divided between bus and rail, Phil Stone was elevated to the position of Deputy Managing Director for the bus side and to keep some balance, Tom Balshaw, formerly an MTL Area Manager, was appointed as my Operations Director. The expectation was that I should relinquish some of my day-to-day control but it did not always work that way.

The Group's Welsh business, Arriva Cymru, was highly dependent on local authority support, as many of the more rural routes in North and Mid-Wales needed subsidy to survive. This meant the Company's financial margins would always be tight and it needed the minimum overhead costs to remain profitable. It was decided that Cymru's accountancy and payroll could be absorbed, with little additional cost, into North West's head office in Aintree but it was suspected by many that this was only a prelude to greater change.

In April 2002 the management of Arriva's interests in Wales was given to the Directors at Aintree and I was suddenly Managing Director of Arriva North West and Wales, responsible for nearly 4,000 personnel at 22 sites spread over an area from Lancashire to Mid-Wales, with a rail franchise on the side.

Comparatively unusual deliveries to Merseyside Transport in 1994 were 13 Auwarter Neoplan integral single-deckers, one of which is photographed in later years in Arriva colours when operating on the 18A Croxteth Park Circular. *(DC)*

Similarly new to Merseyside Transport but seen in Arriva livery is F263 YTJ, one of 20 Leyland Olympians with Northern Counties H47/30F bodies delivered in 1989 and operating on a cross river service through the Mersey tunnel. *(DC)*

Arriva's operations in Manchester had their roots in the establishment of the BeeLine Buzz Company, set up following deregulation and purchased by Drawlane in September 1989. It was operated as a subsidiary of North Western, and the application of the North Western style livery to this Freight Rover, seen here in Piccadilly, is clear. *(JS)*

Double-deckers, such as this former Crosville Leyland Olympian, retained the 'new' company's livery style, but with 'Bee Line' fleet name. *(JS)*

This prompted the appointment of John Rimmer, a devout and trusty manager in Liverpool, to become my second Operations Director, responsible for the English side of the business whilst Tom Balshaw took the Welsh under his wings. With the further present of the depots at Crewe, Winsford and Macclesfield a year later, we had reconstituted the former Crosville Motor Services in nearly all of its manifestations over the previous century. I now had control of the 21st century upgrade of the company that had nurtured and trained me thirty-five years earlier. The influence of Arriva North West and Wales now spread from Aberystwyth to Southport, Anglesey to Crewe. By September 2003 we were preparing budgets for nearly thirty separate locations.

We had seriously wanted to retain the Merseyrail franchise but I could not handle the protracted and complicated process that would lead to our bid when the renewal date approached. I felt it was sensible that I continued to run the franchise on a day-to-day basis whilst others plotted its future. In retrospect, it probably was the wrong course. Neil Scales had succeeded in persuading Central Government that he would make a much better franchising authority than the Strategic Rail Authority and was therefore more influential than ever in determining the ultimate destiny of the franchise. He did not like the members of our bid team and pleaded with me to get involved. I refused and remained detached from the process. We failed to secure the new twenty-five year concession; it went to a Dutch consortium. It was a real disappointment that we were going to be deprived of the opportunity to create a truly integrated bus/rail network.

I am not certain whether I could have influenced the outcome. I am not sure that Neil truly wanted so much power in Arriva's hands but my two years with the rail people had persuaded me that there was a bigger picture to paint here and that bus and rail could be part of the same family. I was touched, when my short tenancy at Rail House came to an end, and my rail directors made a genuinely grateful presentation to me. My views of the rail industry had mellowed and, for a moment, I wondered what might have happened if I had accepted the British Railways traineeship all those years ago.

So I returned to the day job and the vast geography that encompassed the greatly enlarged bus company. The problems were the same as ever, there was just more distance. It was good to re-visit my career 'roots' and staff roadshows and business reviews in the Welsh depots were always lighter than their English equivalents. The Welsh depots' union representatives, however, were, if anything, heavy going. They had immense difficulty in being persuaded that they could not justify the same pay rates and working conditions enjoyed by their Merseyside and Manchester brothers. Although the North Wales coastal routes still generated reasonable profits, they were always dependent on seasonal fluctuations. Most inland routes were dependent on local authority financial support and, with many small family businesses still in the market for tendered work (always with local loyalty), winning and retaining tenders was highly competitive.

The Unions did not want to grasp the reality of the need to remain ahead of the competition and depots like Aberystwyth were always on the edge, awaiting the results of the latest tender round. Our position was not entirely helped by having to deal with so many Local Authorities with differing ambitions and, always, little or no money. In Gwynedd we were up against several small businesses, some of which had been running their local bus service for decades. In Bangor we had competition from a local firm, who seemed to have no idea of the economics of bus operation, but was determined to grab the opportunity to niggle us whenever they could.

Displaying our long-term commitment by building a new depot at Bangor, to replace the ageing buildings on Beach Road, only put more pressure on the finances in that area. During one prolonged wages negotiation, Tom Balshaw and I spent thirteen hours in one session trying to find some compromise. Sometime after nine in the evening, the full-time Union officer shrugged her shoulders and said: "I can't make them (the local reps) see sense". She seemed to think we had some magic formula; all I wanted at that point was my bed.

Across the border our beleaguered attempts to establish ourselves in Warrington finally came to an end with the closure of our depot in the town and the re-distribution of its remaining inter-urban routes to neighbouring depots. This was made slightly easier by our earlier closure of the old Ribble depot in Wigan and the establishment of a new base in Haydock. It had not been without pain, however, as it became the site of my only, albeit half a day, industrial stoppage in thirteen years in the northwest. It is ironic that despite the reputation of unions in Liverpool to the outside world, the relationship at Arriva never resulted in industrial action despite unending wages negotiations, the divestment of Gillmoss and the closure of Huyton depot. The latter did restore a number of routes to the garage at Green Lane, which we had reduced on acquiring MTL. At that time, union relations at Green Lane were not great, engineering standards were poor and we decided that a reduced fleet might also reduce our exposure to any further problems. The gradual re-build did work and we were able to invest in improved engineering facilities and consequently far higher standards all round. Unfortunately, our efforts were not entirely appreciated by one woman.

I first met Beverley Bell in July 2001 shortly after she had been appointed Traffic Commissioner for the North West. The Department for Transport was trying to discard the image that Traffic Commissioners were ex-military types who still expected operators to stand to attention, on parade, when receiving their, usually uninformed, decisions. Lawyers were being recruited to replace the former Army men, but a lady lawyer was met with a certain degree of trepidation. Informally, the small in stature but tall in ambition Mrs Bell genuinely wanted to change the fusty tradition of her predecessors and intended to make a difference. Formally, in her Traffic Court, she assumed the role of headmistress, addressing errant pupils with all the authority she could muster, short of wielding a cane. Our meetings in this forum became all too frequent.

The most notorious of which had followed a period of punctuality monitoring along some of the most heavily bussed corridors in Liverpool. It was clear from the outset that any mitigation we might have for not maintaining our registered timetables was going to fall on deaf ears. At one point I tried to explain that the bus users along Prescot Road, the main corridor linking the centre of Liverpool to St Helens, had little use for timetables as there were over 40 departures an hour and, as Prescot Road was so straight, you could always see the next bus on the horizon. She accused me of 'breath-taking arrogance' a sound-bite much enjoyed in the trade

As explained in the text, Merseyrail essentially comprised two lines; the Wirral line which crossed under the river and then looped around the city centre, as seen in the upper view at Birkenhead, and the Northern line which ran from Southport in the north to Hunts Cross in the south, where in the lower view the third rail electric unit is at Brunswick, the first station south of the city centre. The livery shown was introduced after my departure from Merseyside. *(PA)*

The end of my tenure as Managing Director of Merseyrail was marked by an unexpected presentation by its Chairman.

Thirty Volvo B7TL buses with Alexander 72-seat bodies entered service from Speke garage in 2006 shortly before I was to leave the Merseyside area and return to the Midlands. *(DC)*

press reports of the hearing. Needless to say we lost the case and were fined for our troubles. Perversely, despite my frequent appearances before her, our relationship grew more cordial and, in time, she seemed to recognise that my now lengthening experience in the industry, gave some credibility in policy arguments. In my last appearance in her traffic court, we finally turned the corner from the teacher/pupil relationship.

The services that linked north and south Liverpool by circumventing the City Centre were always prone to disruption. Their problem was that the routes crossed the eleven radial roads serving the City Centre and any one of those could delay buses crossing at those junctions. Despite the PTE's efforts, bus priority had been slow and little of any substance had been achieved to assist these 'cross-city' routes. The results of VOSA's monitoring inevitably resulted in a summons to appear before Mrs Bell.

We went to court armed with PTE representatives who were prepared to offer their support in our contention that we had no control over highway issues and that the effects of congestion on our punctuality were not manageable without the Highways Authority's full commitment. Amazingly, Mrs Bell was not interested in our mitigation but turned her full attention to the PTE people who received the full weight of her lecturing skills on how they had failed miserably in their lack of support for Arriva's long crusade to improve the reliability of its service.

In full flow, she told them that she would pursue them to the ends of the earth to ensure that they raised their game and recognised their responsibilities in providing priority to the bus network. We emerged form her courtroom fully vindicated but totally incredulous. We had witnessed, at last, recognition from the industry's governing body, that bus service unreliability was not always in the control of the operator. This was, without doubt, a significant decision and Mrs Bell perhaps knew that she had rattled the Highways Authority's cage and things would start to take a different course.

The Arriva experience in Manchester had started under the arches at Hulme Hall Road a short distance out of the city centre. The BeeLine Buzz Company was a child of post-deregulation, running transit minibuses in competition with the then PTE-owned bus operator. When Greater Manchester was eventually split in two for privatisation and First Group took the north and Stagecoach the south, things began to get a bit more serious. Much of BeeLine's antics were on the north side of Manchester where its bases in Rochdale and Oldham were in direct competition with some of First's most lucrative routes. However, as First started to get its act together, BeeLine found that running fairly ancient vehicles against a competitor committed to lifting standards, was the recipe for failure. Retrenchment was necessary and sensible so Rochdale and Oldham were closed.

The Starline acquisition in Knutsford opened the south Manchester market and we were able to abandon the damp surrounds of Hulme Hall Road for the former Parcel Force site next to Piccadilly Station. In July 2005 the opportunity arose to expand in North Manchester with the acquisition of Blue Bus of Bolton. The owner, Roger Jarvis, and his two sons had developed the business since 1991 and it looked a good venture. The business was housed in a former Ribble garage that was not the easiest to get in and out. However, we reached a deal and inherited a mixed fleet of around sixty. Unfortunately, the local First Group subsidiary took exception to Arriva's move into their territory and we were faced with renewed competition in North Manchester.

Rodney Dickinson was the Operating Director for First and an easy man to quickly like and do business with. He was also Chairman of the Greater Manchester Travelcard company (GMTL) administered by a former GMPTE employee Jim Hulme. In the mid 'nineties the attempts of the PTE to force through multi-operator travelcards had resulted in the operators coming together under the leadership of Rodney and Jim, to do it themselves. The birth of GMTL was to prove inspirational. In time it provided a template for other areas, but in Manchester it created a legal entity under which operators could meet and jointly provide multi-operator and multi-modal transport. The PTE, at first sceptical, eventually subscribed to the bus operator led concept and became an active, minority participant.

Later, as other issues between the operators and the PTE arose, the operators needed an independent voice away from the ticketing company. This spawned an off-shoot in the Greater Manchester Bus Operators Association (GMBOA), a forum where its members could put forward a united view on transport policy and contribute decisively to the Greater Manchester transport debate. The central plank of that debate was usually the PTE's Metrolink tram system. Most of the bus operators saw this as a real threat, unfairly given priority by the PTE. This came to a head when the authorities announced their intention to ban ordinary traffic, including buses, from the centre of the city but allow unique access for trams. The legal battles that ensured were costly and damaging and although the PTE eventually got its way, the operators did gain concessions elsewhere in the city.

It was an interesting time to take over the Chairmanship of these two bodies, when Rodney announced his decision to stand down. Arriva was still a 'small' company in Manchester terms and I had sat on the GMTL Board as a representative of the small operators. To be unanimously elected by your peers (and competitors) to the chair of GMTL and GMBOA was humbling but also a challenge. Arriva's business in Manchester was not strong and the operators' organisations needed strength and leadership. My five year spell was eventful and certainly challenging. There were constant arguments over concessionary fares reimbursement both for the elderly and children. At times personal relationships with the Executive of the PTE were strained.

Quality Contracts had appeared in the transport lexicon and there were Manchester politicians who believed that the 'cosy' relationship between the operators and the PTE was unhealthy and unnecessary. The PTE's Chief Executive, Chris Mulligan, tried to keep a balance but at times it was an almost impossible task which, ultimately, did not help his own health. But the united voice of the operators' associations was amazingly constant and rarely was there any internal dissent so that the politicians were resigned to some level of respect for the industry. It was draining at times and as my Arriva portfolio broadened, I was happy to pass the mantle over to Stagecoach Manchester's Managing Director Mark Threapleton who proved far more capable than I.

I'm not sure, as life expectancy stretches further each year, whether beginning to feel your age in your mid-fifties is acceptable or just wimpish. I had resisted

Operating from Runcorn depot (what a contrast with those Seddons!) Arriva 2554 (DK55 FYV) was one of a number of VDL Bus SB120s with Wright Cadet bodies delivered to the Liverpool area in 2005. *(DC)*

A trio of all-Scania OmniCity single-deckers was placed in service in 2005, and here the first of them, 2061 (CX05 EOV), is seen operating on the City Centre to John Lennon Airport service. *(DC)*

An annual charity fixture, the Arriva North West Annual Golf Day at Formby always attracted celebrities. Finance Director (and my deputy) Phil Stone, Operations Director Tom Balshaw and Engineering Director Malcolm Gilkerson are joined by Liverpool Football Club legend Kenny Daglish.

Even as a non-golfer I was able to meet my hero.

moving permanently to the North West since David Martin had persuaded me to go there in 1994 and my commuting up and down the unpredictable M6 was becoming more tiresome by the year. I felt that I needed a slightly easier challenge for my last chapter before retirement and the Gods were about to smile on me. However, I was set one more task before I was going to be allowed to step down from the North West and, perversely, it had all the signs of my first experiences with British Bus.

Chester City Transport was an ailing council-owned company where its political owners could see no future that would not come at a cost. The company needed investment, the political will to do so had waned and a sale was now the preferred option. With operations in and surrounding Chester, Arriva wanted to ensure that it would be the preferred bidder for the municipal company and at the same time protect its local interests from an incoming predator. Our view was that any potential buyer would see Chester City as a poor acquisition but its attractiveness was the potential in nearby Wirral and Deeside, predominantly served by Arriva.

First Group was a logical contender but the concern was that others might also spot an opportunity too good to miss. So I was deployed to discuss with officers of the City Council ways of ensuring that Arriva could be in pole position when Chester City Transport was placed on the market. At first the discussions were amicable and the Council officers seemed convinced that Arriva was indeed the most viable option. Unfortunately, when the Council's lawyers became involved, that attitude soon changed and an open sale was more likely to be the outcome.

Rightly or wrongly Arriva decided that it needed some guarantee that a third party would not succeed in beating it to the sale and, as a protection, opted to register the major part of Chester's network. We insisted to the Council that we wanted to secure the best deal for their shareholders, that we would invest in the network and the ageing fleet and we would secure employment. Our estimates were that their bus company was leaking cash and could not survive indefinitely without an injection of financial help. The Council was not in a position to do that and a quick sale was imperative.

The Council's reaction was to threaten legal action on the basis that our actions, to register competitive services, would undermine the sales process and therefore the value of their assets. Within a few weeks our relationship had moved from one of hope for the long-term future of local transport in Chester and the constructive dialogue to achieve that, to 'we'll see you in court'.

The Arriva hierarchy was gathered together for an international conference in Mallorca when we learnt of the City Council's intention to go to the High Court to stop us. Mallorca in September is usually a beautiful place to be, but this time we were accompanied by thunderstorms and torrential flooding that seemed an appropriate backcloth to the news. On our return to the UK we set about the totally absorbing and arduous task of preparing our defence.

The Group engaged Tom Sharpe, an amiable QC with a razor sharp mind and wit. In our preparatory sessions together he was reassuring and confident, although true to his profession was never prepared entirely to commit to the outcome. We arrived at the High Court on 22nd February 2007 and for the next twelve days our actions, or lack of them, as we had not actually introduced any services into Chester by that time, were scrutinised, dissected, challenged and rebuked from all angles.

My two days on the stand started well. The Council's counsel was not as able as Tom and his questioning was not as penetrating as I might have expected. Our problem was The Honourable Mr Justice Rimer.

It was obvious very soon that he thought the Council's case could do with some additional support, and was unforgiving in some of his cross-examination. Tom did everything he could to counter the onslaught but the Judge was determined to have his pound of flesh and saw me as the principal culprit. He was clearly not satisfied that we had proved conclusively that Chester City Transport was on the verge of financial collapse and was not convinced that we had any motive for our intended action that was anything but predatory. At the end of the twelve days, confidence in the chambers of our legal advisors was still relatively high but the potential outcome was always tempered with caution.

When the decision arrived, I received a phone call from one of Tom's associates. The news was good, we had successfully defended our case but I had to prepare myself for the Judge's comments on my evidence. The elation of winning was washed away when I received a copy of the full decision. Despite his conclusion, Mr Justice Rimer made it clear that he had believed very little of my testimony and whilst he just stopped short of calling me a liar, he came remarkably close. The media were kinder in their reporting but even they could not disguise the fact that our success had been gained despite my evidence. We started running local services in Chester; the Council sold its bus company to First Group, and paid Arriva over £1m in costs. A totally stupid outcome to what should have been an easy way to solve and improve on the problems in Chester.

Meanwhile, personnel matters were moving on. Catherine Mason had wanted to replace Steve Clayton as head of Arriva UK Bus when he was elevated to the Arriva Board. An ambitious lady with an extensive marketing background, she believed her experience would lead the Group's bus business, previously so operational led, in a new and exciting direction. Steve's successor was to be a marketer but not Catherine. Mike Cooper came from Easyjet, with a varied and dynamic CV in marketing with household names. The bus business was to be another rung on the ladder of his accelerated career. Inevitably, there was some friction between the marketing talents but Mike was now in charge. Catherine believed or was persuaded that some 'grass roots' operational experience might enhance her CV, which, arguably, it did when she later became Chief Executive of Northern Ireland's transport undertaking, Translink. So when the Managing Director's post in the Midlands subsidiary became vacant, she was the surprising choice.

Midlands was still, in fact, two companies: the east side still traded as Midland Fox and the west side Midlands North. There had been attempts to join the two together but there was still two of everything except at the most senior level. Despite a male-dominated business eying Catherine's appointment with some disbelief, many of her new colleagues quickly warmed to her and although decisions such as unisex toilets in the company's head office gained her some notoriety, she quickly established herself at MD level. Those who were not readily convinced were, almost inevitably, the trade union.

From the Midland Red days, the Leicester based operations had enjoyed a full-time internal union representative. Sam Chapman was the incumbent at the time of Catherine's arrival and Sam was also the Chairman of the Group's National Liaison Committee. Catherine had her ideas about the role of trade unionists and they did not necessarily coincide with those of Sam. The result was that Catherine's Operations Director, Stuart Macintosh, himself a former trade union rep, gained more control through his relationship with the Union which perversely put more pressure on Catherine.

Sadly, the Operations Director unexpectedly died and I was asked to release Tom Balshaw from his duties in Wales to help Catherine. In the meantime union relations in the Midlands had deteriorated quickly. Meetings could not take place without unnecessary numbers from both sides and there were rarely any sensible decisions without external influence. The situation could not endure and David Martin stepped in to extricate Catherine to a more modest role centrally, leaving the question of who would be the sixth Managing Director in ten years to try and moderate the trade union relationships in the Midlands.

An Arriva North West open-topper celebrates, with 500,000 Liverpudlians, the sensational European Cup win in May 2005.

Chapter 8 – Return to the Midlands

I had commuted between our home in Leicester and Merseyside for nearly 13 years. Latterly we had bought an apartment on the Albert Dock in Liverpool which relieved me of the delights of hotel accommodation, but the M6 continued to be a nightmare – my worst recorded time for the 120 mile journey was six and a half hours – and I was ready to start thinking about slowing down a little. My career had gone in cycles of five and eight years (even Merseyside was thirteen) and I was now eight years away from being sixty-five, five years if I opted to retire earlier at sixty-two, which I had always promised myself I would.

Mike Cooper was genuinely taken aback by my request to move back to the Midlands and replace Catherine. A debate ensued whether Phil Stone was ready to return to Liverpool after only three years in Yorkshire. Arriva North West was by now over four times the size of Arriva Yorkshire and whilst Phil's competency was never in doubt, his experience at Managing Director level was still in its infancy. The original plan had been for him to stay there until I was 60 but I was accelerating this by three years.

Steve Clayton came to my aid. His view, very graciously, was, with what I had achieved during my long service, I deserved to make the move, if that was what I wanted. The announcement caused some surprise; there had definitely been a view in many quarters that I would stay in Merseyside until I retired and even the news to my colleagues of Phil's return did not persuade everyone that this was a good move.

However, my leaving was marked by a fine send off at Anfield (where else?) and on 30th July 2007 I put the clock back thirty years to return to what was still Midland Red to me and many others. Tom Balshaw had done a good caretaking job and I know was a little disappointed that he did not have the opportunity to take on the MD role himself. His return to Merseyside was to prove even more momentous.

The art deco façade of the offices at Thurmaston gave some clue that Arriva Midlands was not exactly what it looked like from the outside and, in truth, had a bit of an identity problem. Its head office was located in Leicester. This was the furthest point east of its operations – the company spanned westwards for 102 miles to Oswestry on the Welsh border. And, whilst it pertained to be a Midlands company, in reality it was East Midlands (Leicester – three depots in South Wigston, Southgate Street and Thurmaston; Hinckley, Derby, Swadlincote and Burton-on-Trent) and North Midlands (Cannock, Stafford, Wellington, Shrewsbury and Oswestry).

The city operations in Leicester and Derby were old friends although the network in Leicester was, by now, shared with First who had reduced the former municipality by nearly half since the days of our abortive buy-out attempt. The Derby network, however, was almost identical to the one I had left behind thirteen years earlier and little had changed to the very compact network of routes that still barely strayed more than four miles from the city centre.

My first job was to restore some confidence amongst the management team that was feeling a bit battered from the recent unsettling events. I was, no doubt, seen as a safer pair of hands than my predecessor but I still had to rebuild a sensible working relationship with the Union and all eyes, from all sides, were on how I would approach this. I think I may have met Sam Chapman a couple of times before arriving back in Leicester but I was not altogether ready for the larger than life character that faced me at our first meeting. I recalled a comment John Hargreaves once made to me that there is no such thing as bad union representatives only bad managers. He was right, you get the union reps you deserve and management, if it wants, can steer the relationship to everyone's satisfaction.

It was easy with Sam. He wanted someone who had been around the block a couple of times, someone who would listen and understand, someone who spoke his language and, I suspect, someone who wasn't a woman. I should not have been surprised about his loyalty to the company and his extensive knowledge of the industry and its idiosyncrasies. It took a very short time for us to understand each other and our regular monthly meetings were soon spent more talking about holidays and home life than solving the problems of the day, most of which had already dissipated.

Sam's one major virtue was his honesty. He considered it his duty to deliver, once an agreement had been reached. He was proud of the fact that wage negotiations, which in Merseyside spanned a full calendar year, only took one meeting in the Midlands because the end result had already been agreed between him and me. He was not a 'soft touch'; he had a strong power base at both local and national level and knew what he could deliver and where to draw the line when he could or would not. But he was a realist and when we were faced with closing the depots at Swadlincote and Coalville and severely reducing the size of Stafford, Sam took it upon himself to lead the staff consultations and deliver driver redundancies without any argument or disruption.

The Company started to recognise that the Union was an asset rather than an enemy. We stretched Sam's capabilities and loyalty when we announced the closure of Southgate depot in 2009. The city centre garage was Sam's home depot and we knew the decision to consolidate the Leicester business in the north of the city at Thurmaston and south at Wigston, would be a challenge to deliver. But he did not disappoint and we said goodbye to the depot that had, for so long, been the centre of Midland Red in Leicester and the office in Peacock Lane that I had occupied in 1976, without any hint of resistance.

Arriva Midlands had always delivered a good profit margin but its dependency on its city operations in Leicester and Derby was all too obvious. Much of its territory was semi-rural with a scattering of market towns and often dependent on a large (and unreliable) slug of local authority subsidy. We had to look for places to develop and the glaring hole for Arriva was the West Midlands, still dominated since its privatisation by the National Express subsidiary, Travel West Midlands.

In the first two years of my new tenure we spoke to a number of smaller West Midlands operators to see if we could break into this market by acquisition. Discussions with Hansons in Wordsley and Ludlows in Halesowen came to nought and the latter was subsequently swallowed up by Rotala. A long look at Choice Travel in Wednesfield and a reunion with Julian Peddle could not stack up and I was very disappointed when the Watkiss family, owners of Claribels, a really professional outfit south of Birmingham, could not bring themselves to sell.

We were also suffering from patches of niggling competition. Julian Peddle, for all his business acumen, could not desert his roots in Burton and continued to support Midland Classic who were anything but 'classic' and would not have survived without their patron. A2Z in Walsall was the worst type of operator running low quality vehicles with even lower quality management always just staying one step ahead of the Traffic Commissioners. Arriva Midlands had already had a difficult acquisition of Chase Travel in Cannock to remove a draining competitor and A2Z had simply replaced the problem.

Green Bus in Great Wyrley, despite its local loyalty, was a disgraceful outfit that should not have been allowed to trade. Its owner Graham Martin, by then in his seventies, had lost control of the business and was sitting on one asset – the land that had significant development potential. We visited him with a view to discussing a possible purchase. I had not been to Green Bus before but was warned by my Area Manager, Kevin Walker, that it would be an experience. It was like stepping back forty years. The office was littered with an assortment of ticket machines and equipment and the oldest switchboard – the one with cords and plugs – I had ever seen.

The proprietor, despite his age, chain-smoked and the walls of his office were nicotine yellow. He had ledgers on his desk that had to be accompanied by quill pens but produced no accounts as, in his words, if there was enough money coming in to pay the bills, he was OK. The problem was his fleet, mainly of old Mercedes minibuses, that needed to be scrapped before they finally disintegrated. In the end, to avoid the perils of passive smoking, we left without making an offer and the business was eventually closed by the Traffic Commissioner. That did not prevent a 'phoenix' rising from the ashes of Green Bus, however, and competition in the pretty village of Brewood, north of Wolverhampton continued.

Another major problem for Arriva Midlands had been the lack of investment, particularly in vehicles. My return to Derby 18 years after the employee buy-out, was welcomed, not only by some of my former colleagues, but many of the buses that we had acquired from the City Council. The ghost of British Bus still seemed to haunt the Midlands. Derby was the most profitable depot in Arriva, yet there was still this continuing reluctance to invest. However, in 2008, we were finally able to convince the Board that investment in Derby was too long overdue and the first of sixty-two new buses arrived. Earlier in that year we had also re-equipped Tamworth with a new fleet so the Company had a new spring in its step.

We also had the problems of ageing, in some cases very ageing, depots. The closure of Southgate Street and later Coalville saved us substantial re-building costs on properties that were 82 and 86 years old respectively. These were youngsters, however, when compared to Shrewsbury.

The neighbouring Wellington garage had been in Charlton Street since 1932. It was cramped and dingy and was totally inadequate for the demands of a new town, Telford, which had developed from nowhere in the 1970s. We were desperate to find a new site and resisted spending any kind of money on the present location's upkeep. The consequences were regular power failures (the electrical wiring resembled strands of unruly spaghetti creeping ivy-like around the walls), eroded masonry clinging to window frames and a generally damp and insecure

My 40th anniversary in the industry was celebrated with a cartoon depicting my legendary appearances before the Traffic Commissioner, my love of football, my doubtful computer skills, my reputation for speeding and treasured memories of conducting.

One of the newest vehicles delivered to Derby at the time of my retirement was this Optare Versa, No. 2948 (YJ61 CFF) operating on a service dating back to the Corporation provision of services. *(DC)*

Also seen in Derby is Scania OmniCity No. 3569 (YT09 ZBO), one of 26 such vehicles delivered to Arriva for operation in that town in 2008/9. *(DC)*

Eighteen years after the Derby buy-out my return to the Midlands found some of that fleet still in service. However, in 2008 a new fleet was launched in the City, with appropriate ceremony taking place at Derby County's new ground. Well, we could hardly do it at Anfield, could we? A nocturnal view finds me posing with both new buses and football ground behind me. *(DC)*

working area that barely acknowledged 21st century Health and Safety standards. Eventually, and not before time, we found an ideal site in Stafford Park, a large industrial estate only five minutes away from Telford Bus Station, the centre of the local bus network. The unit was to be vacated by a contracting haulier and we did not think planning permission would be a problem. We were right but the legal wranglings over the site took nearly two years to resolve so that it was not until early 2012 that we finally made the move.

The saga of Shrewsbury depot was even more long running. The site had stood, just north of the town centre, on the A5191 at Springfield Gardens since 1912. It literally stood adjacent to the main Shrewsbury to Whitchurch road and incredibly this meant that vehicles had to reverse off the main road to be fuelled when they returned to the depot each night. How we, and our predecessors, had been allowed to make these manoeuvres for so long without challenge defies belief. Again we were desperate to re-locate, but the present site was not big and poorly located so was unlikely to be very valuable when vacated. Half of Shrewsbury's business was dependent on subsidy so it had little chance of supporting or warranting substantial re-development costs.

Neighbouring the garage was an old flax mill that the local council was keen to develop into a visitor attraction and apartments. Much to our relief the council placed a compulsory purchase order on the depot in 2006 and we began the process of persuading the council to pay for our relocation. The protracted negotiations took five years until the first sod was finally cut at our new site at Battlefield, three miles out of Shrewsbury. Within a year we were in our new eco-friendly premises, light years away from Spring Gardens and from reversing on and off main roads.

The news in late 2010 that Arriva had been acquired by the German state-owned, Deutsche Bahn (DB) caused more than a few raised eyebrows. Industry thinking had been that consolidation was inevitable amongst the 'big groups' and that Go Ahead and National Express would probably be the first to succumb to foreign ownership. Like all of the big five, Arriva needed investment and David Martin was canny enough to know that this was not going to come from conventional methods. DB, on the other hand, had logistical interests across twenty-five countries but their German home power base was vulnerable. Liberalisation was coming and their rail monopoly would face competition in the near future.

Arriva was the perfect vehicle to develop the DB business outside Germany. It had already amassed bus and rail businesses across ten European states and its acquisitory reputation and success rate was worth buying. The irony of being state owned, albeit by the German Bundestag, did not escape our peers and even the former Deputy Prime Minister John Prescott could not resist poking fun at a Confederation of Passenger Transport annual dinner. There was little doubt, however, that the Group's buying power had suddenly improved and a new era of development was about to begin.

Initially, there was very little evidence of our new owners and the senior Arriva directors managed to keep DB at arms length. The UK bus industry was a bit of a mystery to our German colleagues. They understood and felt comfortable with the London bus model and rail franchising but the free-for-all deregulated market, albeit twenty-five years old, did not conform to any of their structures. Gradually we were invited to start our rehabilitation, by attending grand DB conferences in Frankfurt and Berlin that usually comprised of 45 Arriva and nearly 1,100 DB personnel. The DB mantra was entirely size dependent. They were big and wanted to be the biggest.

After the initial apprehension and, it has to be said, a degree of fear, the DB acquisition began to generate confidence and even in their small outpost in Leicester, we were feeling a bit more adventurous. UK bus had begun to realise that bus operations alone did not offer long-term viability and some degree of diversification was necessary. It would be very easy to get involved in businesses that were totally alien to the expertise that existed in the Group. Many had trodden that uncertain path before and many had failed, but a serious appraisal of the opportunities that involved wheels started to point us towards Social Services and non essential patient transport, the latter proving to be a far bigger market than we had ever imagined. Jonathan May, my colleague in the North East, was deployed to explore the potential of these markets but there was still an underlying resistance to this step into the unknown.

A family-owned company in Stoke on Trent gave us the push we needed. Wardles had been shrewdly built by Doug Wardle and his family over a period of nearly fifty years. To the outside world it looked a bit of a hotchpotch, but a mixture of local bus services, some commercial, some Council-supported, private hire, Social Services and NHS contracts nicely spread the risk and avoided dependency on one discipline. We had looked at Wardles a couple of years earlier but had decided that, at sixty miles from Thurmaston, it was a little remote (regardless of the fact that Oswestry was 102 miles away!) In truth, we were also concerned about the reaction from First Bus who were the principal operator in that area. Now it offered the opportunity to test diversification and get us recognised in the new markets.

Our first visit to the Wardles base in Burslem could have changed our minds. The operations were located on two sites, not adjoining and both resembling a council refuse tip. The offices were depressing and whilst the fleet was generally in good condition, it was difficult to see how they were properly maintained. As ever, the proprietor thought his business to be perfect and worth considerably more than we were prepared to pay, but he was ready to retire so the usual 'shadow boxing' took its course and eventually a deal was done.

Shortly before Christmas 2010 we completed the acquisition, met the staff and started to discover what we had let ourselves in for. It was exciting and challenging but we had inherited a capable manager, Keith Stanton, who knew his way around and was soon able to help Jonathan May with the Group's greater goals. What was clear from the outset was that we needed better premises and for all the business to be on one site. Although Doug owned one of the facilities, the other was leased from a dubious absentee Spanish landlord. The documentation attached to this lease was sparse to say the least and felt very uncomfortable. We were therefore determined to find our way out at the earliest opportunity.

In the event, the answer was not far away. The other local operator was D&G run by Dave Reeves with considerable support, moral and financial, from Julian Peddle. D&G ran from a purpose built site about 4 miles from the Wardles base and a consolidation of both companies' businesses seemed to be the solution. This

The first of 18 26-seat Optare Solos, No. 2905 (YJ58 CCA) also participated in the launch of the new fleet in Derby and is seen here at Pride Park. *(DC)*

As in Merseyside, Arriva Midlands also had some Scania OmniCities in a dedicated route livery. In this case the service is the X31 between Cannock and Birmingham, the antecedents of which were inherited when Midland Red took over the Heath Hayes based Harpers Brothers operation. *(DC)*

meant extended negotiations with Julian, always entertaining, often frustrating, but a deal was eventually struck and in August 2011 we took over the D&G business in Stoke and, more importantly, their premises in Longton.

Despite the acres of space we had acquired the engineering accommodation was still limited and basic. The combined fleet was now almost a hundred vehicles and, although there was some opportunity to consolidate we were desperate for better engineering facilities. Dave Reeves had retained ownership of the depot and he was persuaded to extend the building that, while simple in its conception, took six months to complete. In the meantime, we were now trying to run the two businesses from three sites and that took its toll. Stoke on Trent Council, like so many Local Authorities, were desperate for financial savings and decided to withdraw totally their support to the network of local services. This hit the newly expanded Wardles hard and made it more urgent that we achieved economies of scale.

Our experiences in the Potteries did not deter us from looking for further expansion and once again our thoughts turned to the West Midlands. The tender market itself was worth millions and, apart from some peripheral involvement in Cannock, we had not ventured seriously into its core. Arriva Midlands needed part of that action and as our attempts to acquire our way into that market had been unsuccessful, the only other means of entry was to set up a base from where we could compete for this tender work. There were plenty of sites available but we really needed a ready-made depot that we could lease, initially short term, to minimise our risk.

The answer was at Hill Top, just north of my hometown of West Bromwich. I had come full circle. The depot had had a history of occupants and was now in the hands of Go Ahead after their abortive and very expensive excursion into the West Midlands. The building was cavernous; it would easily accommodate seventy vehicles but we were looking for twenty vehicles maximum so we agreed to lease the front part with the option of expanding when the necessity arose.

To say that our colleagues at West Midlands PTE (Centro) were pleased with our decision was an understatement. They had long tried to persuade us to enter the tender market, which had been dominated by Travel West Midlands and now we were here. But we had to win the tenders. Now that we had a base, we felt more confident about competing fairly aggressively for the work and our determination paid off early in 2012. In fact we won too much work and had to persuade the PTE to take some back when it was apparent that the eight weeks we had to get the depot up and running would limit our opportunity to be selective in our recruitment.

With a monumental effort, just about everything came together in April 2012 and we were operating a disparate selection of routes in the West Midlands. We had been told that the next big tender round was to take place in Sandwell (West Bromwich) and we were now ideally placed to compete for that work. However, the PTE's timetable began to slip and our expansion plan was in danger of disintegrating at birth. The answer, again, came from the Julian Peddle/Dave Reeves partnership. D&G, as Choice Travel, had a depot in Wednesfield, a few miles southeast of Wolverhampton. We had looked at this company before but could not make a bid stack up. Choice had built a 60 vehicle business from tenders and some commercial work and that would give us the volume we were now needed. For the second time

The family owned business of Wardle Transport based in Stoke on Trent was acquired by Arriva in 2010. The upper view shows Dennis Dart SLF, No. 2301 (OUI 9120).with Marshall B39F body. The lower view depicts an Optare Versa, with 38 seats, No. 2962 (WT58 BUS), which was purchased new in 2008. *(DC both)*

Shrewsbury Depot was the Midland Red garage at Ditherington which had opened in November 1920, replacing two earlier garages. It was a fine example of early BMMO buildings.

My final duties at the opening of the new Arriva Midlands depot at Shrewsbury with Transport Minister Norman Baker.

in a year I sat down with my Financial Director, John Barlow, to spar with Julian and Dave and though we inevitably reached agreement, I would not be there to see its conclusion.

The move to Leicester had certainly brought its compensations. The treks up and down the M6 were now a distant memory, having an office 15 minutes from home started to give a better and more realistic work/life balance. Barbara and I had decided to buy a bolthole in Mallorca, a place we first visited during our twenty-fifth anniversary year, although it had taken a further eleven years to make that decision.

Tony Williamson, who had been Arriva's MD in Scotland in the late 'nineties, had moved to the Mainland Europe team and had become responsible for the Group's Iberian acquisitions. He had actually started his working life as an apprentice mechanic at Leicester City Transport when I had been there. Bravely, he had uprooted his wife Beverley and their three children who were now enjoying life in Mallorca. The Williamson family were keen to show us the benefits of the Spanish way of life and were a source of much knowledge (and best places to eat) that prompted our thoughts on a retirement strategy that would involve more time in the sunshine. Our holiday home gave us the opportunity to develop friendships that would make a more regular transition easier, so we grasped every opportunity to be on the island, facilitated by a two hour flight from East Midlands Airport with either Easyjet or Ryanair.

Four events in 2010 had made me think seriously about my future. In July I reached my sixtieth birthday, a date that I had always anticipated would be a good time to finish. I saw no merit in battling on to the conventional retirement age of sixty-five; I had seen too many colleagues fail to reach retirement and some who did, lost the strength to survive long afterwards. I was uncertain how I would cope with making such a decision and what the aftermath would hold for me but I knew that I would need time to get my head round leaving the industry that had been my life. The three other events put my qualms into perspective.

Barbara was diagnosed with a tumour on her liver and we suffered several weeks of uncertainty until an operation removed half of her liver and her gall bladder but she was given the all clear. In such times it is inevitable to think about the true values of life and not necessarily the material ones. We had been married for forty years; she had supported me throughout, even when she did not fully agree with me, and perhaps the time had come to repay some of that loyalty.

And then in June Malcolm Gilkerson, for long my Engineering Director at Aintree, died. I was on my way to visit him when the I got the news and whilst he had been ill for some time, he had never fully recovered from a motorcycle accident he had had some years previous, it was still a great shock. Malcolm was a good engineer, devoted to his work and devoutly loyal. He would easily get frustrated when things weren't going his way and his powers of communication often abandoned him. But he had a big heart and his untimely death at fifty-six still seems unfair. My lasting memory of him was his appearance at Aintree one day in full motor cycling leathers and helmet (his motorcycle was his great love and responsible for many speeding fines) when someone remarked that he looked like Darth Vader!

Within a month, a second of my former Directors was also dead. Tom Balshaw had become a close friend as well as a loyal colleague since the Merseybus take-over. His brain tumour, diagnosed eighteen months earlier, had been a great shock and as everyone prayed optimistically for his full recovery, his gradual deterioration had been painful to watch. To lose two colleagues that had been part of my Liverpool team during the most successful time in my own career was sobering and tragic.

There is no guarantee of long life but I had always felt I would like the luxury of deciding when I wanted to finish work rather than the decision being imposed on me. In January 2011, during my annual review with Mike Cooper, I shocked him for the second time by my decision to retire when I reached sixty-two in the summer of the following year. I gave twelve months formal notice that summer, twice what I was required to do, but to give Mike adequate time to sort out my successor and, more importantly, for me time to acclimatise to being unemployed forever.

As I have recorded, activity in the final eighteen months did not abate but when July 2012 finally arrived, I was as prepared as I could ever be for this irreversible decision. At a lunch held in Liverpool, attended by about eighty of my friends and colleagues, some of whom had been around from the beginning, Clive Myers and David Martin, bosses from either end of my career, were warm and kind in their recognition of my achievements. There was one absentee: John Hargreaves was, by then, too frail to travel but wrote to me with typical advice on how to succeed in retirement and to tell me that he had never been angry about my defection to Leicester City, he had only been concerned about my future. My guardian angel had been there to the end.

My friends and colleagues generously celebrated my departure to the point when, after a very pleasant lunch with the Midlands trade union representatives and Directors, I had had enough farewells and slipped away three days before my official retirement date. I had worked in the bus industry for forty-four years and twenty-four days and it had given me everything. It is easy to remember the good times and there were certainly low points, but I cannot look back without a sense of satisfaction and fulfilment. I had witnessed and had been a very small part of major changes in how this country provides its public transport. The industry has survived the turmoil of deregulation and privatisation and is a shadow of what it was when I first encountered it as a naive seventeen year old. But it is still vibrant, it still has those with the enthusiasm to face the future and one day, it may be recognised as the integral part of a successful economy, which it has always tried to be.

Postscript

So, can someone so absorbed with this industry for a lifetime spanning six decades survive without it? Well, perhaps yes, perhaps no. The early days of my retirement were happily spent in our second home in Mallorca and the summer proved a good time of the year to change our life. But as usual, Barbara knew that I would have to have something to focus on and whilst swimming, walking, a very healthy lifestyle and two beautiful grandchildren were to be appreciated, I would need something else.

I have always enjoyed reading and always fancied writing but I am not sure that I was ever destined to be a great novelist or had the confidence to try. Writing about something on which I have a little experience and knowledge was an obvious extension, so I set to paper some reminiscences of my early years of bus travel which Alan Millar, the Editor of 'Buses' magazine, was kind enough to print. This was the encouragement I needed to develop my journalistic skills in relatively safe territory. My life to date has been full of bus stories and now, perhaps, I can share them with others and keep a link, that has been such a part of my life, without any of the responsibilities! Perhaps Hindsight will prove an invaluable characteristic in my new career.

December 2016

This final picture brings the photographic coverage of my career to a conclusion. Seen in the very heart of Birmingham in CityLinx livery is one of the newest Volvo B9TL with Wrght Eclipse Gemini body, No.4206 (FJ08 LVS).*(DC)*